# University of Pennsylvania

# University of Pennsylvania

AN ARCHITECTURAL TOUR BY
George E. Thomas

PHOTOGRAPHS BY
Lewis Tanner and George E. Thomas

FOREWORD BY
Titus D. Hewryk

Princeton Architectural Press
NEW YORK | 2002

This book has been made possible through the generous support
of the Graham Foundation for Advanced Studies in the Fine Arts.

Princeton Architectural Press
37 East Seventh Street
New York, New York 10003

For a free catalog of books, call 1.800.722.6657.
Visit our web site at www.papress.com.

SERIES EDITOR: Jan Cigliano
SERIES CONCEPT: Dennis Looney
PROJECT EDITOR: Nicola Bednarek
DESIGN: Sara E. Stemen
MAPS: Jane Sheinman
SPECIAL THANKS TO: Nettie Aljian, Ann Alter, Amanda Atkins, Janet Behning,
Megan Carey, Penny Chu, Clare Jacobson, Mark Lamster, Nancy Eklund Later,
Linda Lee, Lottchen Shivers, Katharine Smalley, Scott Tennent, Jennifer Thompson, and
Deb Wood of Princeton Architectural Press          —Kevin C. Lippert, publisher

LIBRARY OF CONGRESS CATALOGING-IN-PUBLICATION DATA
Thomas, George E.
    University of Pennsylvania / George E. Thomas ; photographs by Lewis
Tanner ; foreword by Titus D. Hewryk—1st ed.
        p. cm.—(The campus guide)
Includes bibliographical references (p.   ) and index.
    ISBN 1-56898-315-8
    1. University of Pennsylvania—Buildings—Guidebooks.  2. University of
Pennsylvania—Buildings—Pictorial works.  I. Tanner, Lewis.  II. Title.  III. Campus
guide (New York, N.Y.)
    LD4531 .T58 2002
    378.748′11—dc21
                        2001006163

PRINTED IN CHINA

## CONTENTS

This guide book is intended for visitors and members of the university community who wish to enjoy the principal buildings of our campus, from Frank Furness's fiery red library to the serene quiet of Wilson Eyre's University Museum or the extroverted modernism of Venturi, Scott Brown and Associates' brilliant remaking of Perelman Quadrangle and associated buildings. The streets that border our campus and our principal walks and lawns are all open to the public as are many of our buildings which could reasonably be expected to serve the public, including restaurants, stores, museums, galleries, libraries, concert halls, theaters, and similar facilities. Some, such as archives and special collections, may require advance appointments. If in doubt, please call ahead. Facilities devoted to research, residence, and classrooms are primarily private though visible from the campus and often may be visited with advance preparation.

Our book is organized into six campus tours, or "Walks," as well as a more generalized overview of architectural treasures of the neighborhood. Each Walk is organized by a historical overview and an aerial perspective map that identifies the buildings covered in each Walk. The map is followed by short texts and photographs of the buildings and open spaces that are featured in the separate sections. The last tour is more general and is probably best done with an automobile. It includes notable sites in the Penn neighborhood such as the landmark churches and railroad terminal, Drexel University's main building, and Frank Furness's Centennial Bank, now Drexel's Peck Center. Sites related to Penn's history across the larger city are also covered, including such Penn landmarks as the Mask and Wig Club and the Morris Arboretum in Chestnut Hill.

Because so many of our leaders and architects are Penn alumni, we have indicated that in the text. The first date given is the year of graduation from the College. Where relevant, the second date and professional degrees are indicated. Thus, when referring to Provost Pepper (1843–1898; 1862, M.D. 1864) indicates a member of the College class of 1862 and a medical degree two years later.

**University of Pennsylvania buildings that are regularly open to the public include:**
The Admissions Office in College Hall
The Annenberg Center for specific performances

The Fisher Fine Arts Library with the Architectural Archives and
the Arthur Ross Gallery
Houston Hall market and shops
The Institute of Contemporary Art
Irvine Auditorium for performances
The Moravian Café
The Penn Bookstore and restaurants of the Inn at Penn
The University Museum
Van Pelt Library

Dates and times of special events and exhibitions can be found on
the University of Pennsylvania web site and in the university's student
newspaper, *The Daily Pennsylvanian*, as well as in local newspapers.

**For further information, please contact:**
The University of Pennsylvania
34th and Walnut streets
Philadelphia, PA 19104
(215) 898 5000
www.upenn.edu

## Acknowledgments

As in any such project, we have depended on the support and assistance of the University of Pennsylvania's Facilities staff, the University Archives and Records Center as well as the architects and planners who continue to embellish our campus. They have provided timely information and images that have enriched our portrait of the university as it is in 2001.

The book is a testament to the University of Pennsylvania's leaders, especially President Judith S. Rodin, Provost Robert L. Barchi, Executive Vice President John A. Fry, and Vice President for Facilities and Real Estate Services Omar Blaik, who have built upon the university's previous 130 years of design in West Philadelphia and now have extended its influence into the neighboring community, thereby recognizing our mutual dependency and offering an important vision for the urban university. This book salutes their efforts.

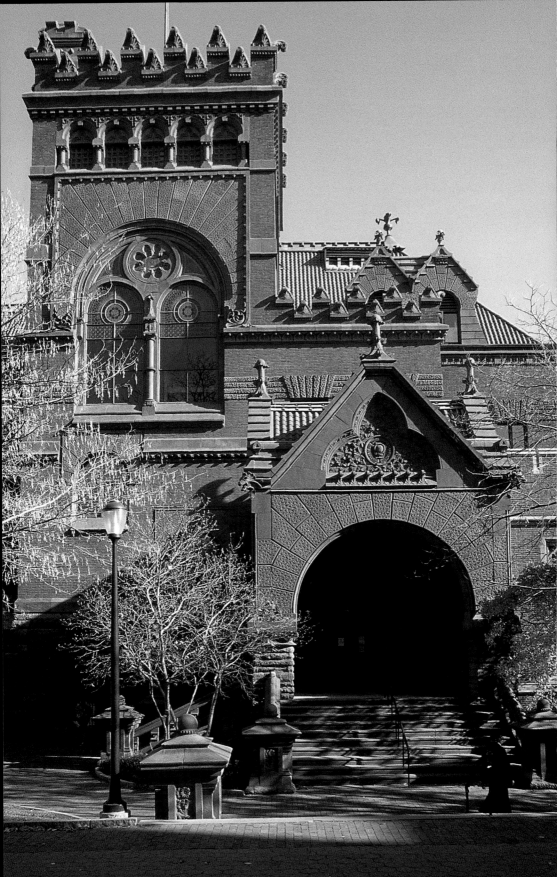

## PLANNING THE MODERN UNIVERSITY

This book is both a field guide to the University of Pennsylvania campus and a celebration of the campus's architecture and open spaces. Buildings of all styles and periods from the 1870s to the present are described. The guide does not limit itself to the narrow confines of the boundaries of the university's third campus but also includes major architectural landmarks of the surrounding neighborhoods that are viewed as important assets that enhance the institution. George Thomas, a longtime resident of West Philadelphia's University City, co-author of a recent work on Penn's campus, veritable enthusiast of Philadelphia's architectural history, and a lecturer in the university's Historic Preservation and Urban Studies programs, provides the reader with a historical overview and commentary on Penn's architectural treasures. As University Architect, I have taken this opportunity to introduce the reader to the planners and planning processes that have shaped Penn's past five decades of dramatic growth, which in turn provide the framework and stimuli for the development of the present-day campus.

The University of Pennsylvania's modern campus is largely a result of the unprecedented growth after World War II that transformed an old but moderately scaled regional university into an internationally renowned institution. Planning work on the campus expansion commenced during the immediate post-war years. At that time university trustees considered, but subsequently rejected, the possibility of relocating the entire institution from West Philadelphia to a then rural site on the edge of George Washington's winter camp at Valley Forge. In 1948, the Philadelphia City Planning Commission certified the university area to be a part of the city's Urban Renewal Program. In the same year a Plan of Development was published, representing ideas of the beaux-arts–trained design faculty of the university. Some of its elements were later incorporated into University City's Urban Renewal Plan. It was during this time that the idea of Locust Street as a tree-lined pedestrian walk closed to vehicular traffic was initially proposed. The Plan of Development also recommended the demolition of many of the university's historic buildings, including the old University Library designed in the 1890s by Frank Furness—the now renowned but then reviled Victorian architect.

The first campaign for campus development commenced in the early 1950s under the leadership of President Gaylord P. Harnwell, Provost David Goddard, and G. Holmes Perkins, former chairman of the Planning Department at Harvard University and then dean of Penn's Graduate School of Fine Arts. At that time, Perkins was also chairman of the City Planning Commission, participating in the larger planning issues of the entire city. As a prelude to its rapid growth, the university undertook an educational survey, its first self-analysis study in nearly half a century. Funded by the Ford Foundation and led by Dr. John H. Willetts, it recommended the establishment of the position of Vice President for Coordinated Planning and the organization of the university's first Planning Office. These offices were headed respectively by John C. Heatherston and Harold Taubin.

In early 1961, the report "An Element of the Continuing Planning Program—University of Pennsylvania Development Plan" was submitted to President Harnwell and subsequently approved by the university's Board of Trustees. In February 1963, the updated "University Campus Development Plan" was presented to the Philadelphia City Planning Commission and to the Philadelphia Redevelopment Authority. A year later it was approved by the Philadelphia City Council. In 1965, Philadelphia's Urban Renewal Program for University City and Penn's Institutional Development District was established, and by the fall of 1966, the University of Pennsylvania's "Campus Development Plan—1975" was completed.

The drafts of the 1966 Campus Development Plan envisioned the university as it would be in the middle of the next decade. It established guidelines for the future general land use and open spaces of the campus, the location of proposed buildings, their projected size, and their relationship with each other. Among the goals of the Campus Development Plan were the desire to convey to the coming generation of students a legacy of inspiration, beauty, order, and efficiency and the development of a residential campus of "internal unity and external identification." The proposal for the campus circulation system called for a pedestrian-oriented complex of buildings unified within major and minor open spaces and by connecting pedestrian walks. Its central idea was the conversion of Locust Street into an east-west pedestrian walk that would tie together the rapidly growing campus. Finally, the authors of the Campus Development Plan anticipated a rise in student enrollment from 16,800 in 1961–1962, to 22,000 in 1970–1971. Remarkably, most of these ideas came to pass—though in the charged political environment of the late 1960s and early 1970s, which saw top-down planning disrupted and transformed by student demonstrations and sit-ins.

As the 1960s ended, implementation of the 1975 Campus Development Plan recommendations was in full swing. The city's Redevelopment Authority acquired by eminent domain and subsequently conveyed to the university most of the present-day campus northwest of Woodland Avenue as far as 40th Street. Woodland Avenue itself, Locust Street, and portions of 36th, 37th, and 39th streets were stricken from city maps and closed to vehicular traffic. On some blocks wholesale demolition of nineteenth-century and early twentieth-century buildings took place. Campus buildings lost at that time included such landmarks as the Robert Hare Hall (1877, Thomas W. Richards) on the corner of 36th and Spruce Street and the John Harrison Laboratory of Chemistry (1894, Cope and Stewardson) on Spruce and 34th streets. West of 38th Street numerous

handsome Victorian mansions met a similar fate. At the same time, dozens
of new buildings were built. Architectural firms with political connections to
the state were commissioned to design most of these buildings. Their construction was partially subsidized by the Commonwealth's General State
Authority. By July 1968, thirty major facility projects were under design or
construction, at a total cost of approximately $130 million. In less than
twenty years, Penn spent over $200 million and more than doubled its gross
building area.

The building boom of the late 1960s and early 1970s produced a
landscape where new structures were surrounded by patched-up concrete,
asphalt walks, and eroded bits of grass, interspersed with sidewalk curbs and
remnants of trolley tracks from the closed streets. To celebrate Penn's new
campus, buildings were designed to face toward interior courts and away
from the perimeter streets. As a result, the public face of the university was
the backs of new buildings such as Van Pelt Library, the Annenberg Center,
and the Social Sciences complex. This planning policy separated Penn from
the city and created generally barren streetscapes.

By the middle of the 1970s, the bulk of the university's building
expansion was completed, but most areas of the enlarged campus grounds
were in disrepair. With the exception of the 3600 block of Locust Street,
which was converted into a pedestrian walk by landscape architect George
Patton, no major landscaping or replanting efforts were undertaken.
Fortunately, in the mid-1970s, stimulated by the public intervention of Ian
McHarg—Penn's renowned landscape architect and planner and chairman of
Penn's Landscape Architecture and Regional Planning Department—
President Martin Meyerson authorized the development of the Campus
Landscape Master Plan. Vice President Fred Shabel wholeheartedly sup-
ported this endeavor. In the summer of 1976, the Center for Environmental
Design directed by Sir Peter Shepheard, dean of the Graduate School of
Fine Arts, commenced work on a plan for Penn's landscape. Thanks to Fred
Shabel's support and the magnificent gift of patron and Penn friend Blanche
Levy, the dilapidated remnants of the old street network between College
Hall and Van Pelt Library were transformed into Blanche Levy Park. The
new landscape was an instant success. One of the testimonies of Blanche
Levy Park's triumph is that new generations of students and faculty perceive
it as the "historic" center of the campus.

During the past twenty years, the landscape vocabulary developed by
Sir Peter Shepheard's team of faculty and students has been slowly and carefully extended across the surrounding area, which is now known as the "historic core of the campus": the section encompassed by 33rd to 38th, and Spruce
to Walnut streets. More recently, thanks to individual class gifts and the support of numerous campus friends, the landscape vocabulary of Blanche Levy
Park has been extended to include the Law School's interior courtyard, Bower
Field, the garden of the President's House, and the Inn at Penn.

In spring 1999 the university's Board of Trustees approved the formulation of the Campus Development Plan that would establish new principles to guide the university's future growth. The landscape architecture and urban design firm Olin Partnership was commissioned to serve as the primary planning consultant. Significantly, its two principals, Laurie Olin and Susan Weiler, are long-term residents of University City, and Laurie Olin was one of the faculty members of Sir Peter Shepheard's team that produced the Landscape Development Plan of the mid-1970s. The stated purpose of the new Campus Development Plan was to ensure that the university's physical environment fulfilled the academic and research goals that were articulated in President Judith Rodin's "Agenda for Excellency."

With the enthusiastic support and under the leadership of Provost Robert L. Barchi, Executive Vice President John Fry, and Vice President for Facilities and Real Estate Services Omar Blaik, the "Campus Development Plan—2001" has been completed. It is the result of a comprehensive consultative process in which five working committees composed of faculty, staff, and students collaborated with the planning consultants. In spring 2001, the plan was approved by the Board of Trustees. Based on key findings of the two-year planning study, it contains the following goals and recommendations: to strengthen connections between the various campus areas and the historic core, to extend the character and amenities of the historic core across the entire campus, to reinforce the historic core bounded by 33rd and 38th, Walnut and Spruce streets; to encourage rehabilitation and adaptive reuse of existing buildings, to connect the campus to the Center City, and to support the preservation and enhancement of University City's residential communities.

At present the university and its affiliated institutions are engaged in another round of construction, which will continue their growth and the transformation of the region. Under Vice President John Fry's leadership, the university is formulating plans for the completion of Penn's retail district and the development of the area between the river and the present-day campus. As a prelude to the latter, the former Pennsylvania Railroad Freight Station at Walnut and 31st streets was recently converted into an upscale apartment building. Kohn Pedersen Fox Associates is enlarging the Wharton School campus with a structure that by itself encompasses more space than the entire Victorian campus of the 1880s. On the 40th Street edge, Carlos Zapata has designed a cinema, retail, and parking complex that is now being completed. The School of Dental Medicine is completing construction of a Bohlin Cywinski Jackson–designed clinic addition. In the heart of the campus, the engineering school has just commenced construction of a Kieran Timberlake Associates–designed research building. Construction also commenced on the David S. Pottruck Health and Fitness Center. The University Museum is completing the Atkin, Olshin, Lawson-Bell–designed Mainwaring Wing for collections storage. The medical campus is planning new laboratories and garages in the former Civic Center area, and Children's

*Entrance to Facilities Offices, 3101 Walnut Street, MGA Partners, 2000*

Hospital is wrapping its 1970s building with a new facade by Kohn Pedersen Fox Associates and is adding new towers to its campus. The campus landscape vocabulary is being extended, new student housing is being planned, and the Quad is being renovated and relandscaped. In short, life continues as it has for the past half century.

Penn prides itself on being what some visitors describe as one of the greener places among America's urban campuses. With this in mind, it is useful to recall Sir Peter Shepheard's words in his introduction to Penn's mid-1970s Landscape Development Plan: "We start with the idea that the purpose of a university campus is to provide a setting for the life of the university. Much of that life of course takes place in buildings and its richness depends on the quality of these buildings. But there is also a large part which goes on outside buildings, in the landscape. The daily passage of people in the landscape should provide a nexus of meeting, of recreation, or merely of relaxation, all of which greatly enrich university life. If a campus has an image in the mind as a place to be loved and admired, it is likely to be formed not so much by the buildings as by the spaces in between."

Titus D. Hewryk
University Architect
University of Pennsylvania

1755

1782

1882

1884

1893

1894

1895

1900

# Introduction

Half a century ago the Ivy League was established, linking eight of the nation's oldest and most prestigious eastern universities. By age, the University of Pennsylvania was in the middle third of its peer institutions, but as the southernmost of the group, it was peripheral in location. Moreover, it was very different in the nature of its campus, which was urban, fragmented, and lacking the patina of age of its rivals because its oldest buildings had been left behind in two previous moves. Penn was also different in focus. Unlike its New England counterparts located in the nation's intellectual heartland, the university's Philadelphia setting placed it in an industrial center which valued applied research. In 1946, that ethos bore fruit at Penn's Moore School of Electrical Engineering with the construction of ENIAC, the world's first electronic computer. In the intervening half century, Penn's leaders have learned to value their progressive heritage while they have transformed the campus and the institution into the global center of education and research that it is today.

## Beginnings

When Benjamin Franklin founded the Academy and Charitable School of Philadelphia in 1749, he set the American course for higher education as a secular rather than a religiously centered enterprise. The separation between college and church was made possible by the peculiar circumstances of Philadelphia, which was founded by members of the Religious Society of Friends (Quakers). Since the Friends' meeting for worship did not require ministers, the typical reason for founding a college was precluded. Philadelphia's college was established more than a century after the founding of Puritan Harvard College and nearly half a century after that of the Puritan New Haven and Anglican Williamsburg colleges.

In his *Autobiography*, Franklin remembered that he first conceived of the college in 1745, but other events occupied his time and he did not act until several years later. The seeds of the institution that is now the University of Pennsylvania were sown in 1749 when Franklin published *Proposals Relating to the Education of Youth in Pensilvania, Philadelphia: Printed in the*

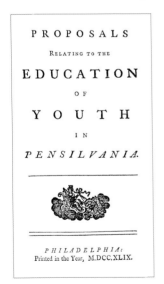

PROPOSALS

RELATING TO THE

EDUCATION

O F

YOUTH

I N

PENSILVANIA.

PHILADELPHIA:
Printed in the Year, M.DCC.XLIX.

*Benjamin Franklin*, Proposals Relating to the Education of Youth in Pensilvania. *Philadelphia, 1749*

*Year MDCCXLIX.* This tract rallied supporters who raised capital, established a Board of Trustees presided over by Franklin, and purchased a building under his direction. Franklin's proposal was remarkable for its originality, perhaps because he himself had not attended any of the New England institutions of higher education. Instead of focusing on ancient languages and traditional subjects such as theology and law, he intended to create an institution that would serve the needs of the present by offering courses in modern languages and the newly evolving natural sciences, as well as teaching skills needed for the emerging professions. To this end he suggested that the new institution be built in the city rather than in rural isolation and, most remarkably, called for the rector to be a "correct and pure Speaker and Writer of the *English* tongue . . ." The courses would be taught in the secular language of the day rather than an ecclesiastical language of the past.

He also proposed a program of athletic exercises focusing on his favorite activities such as running and swimming. Franklin's thoughts on the curriculum were among the most advanced of his day:

> As to their Studies, it would be well if they could be taught *every Thing* that is useful and *every Thing* that is ornamental: But Art is long and their Time is short. It is therefore propos'd that they learn those Things that are likely to be *most useful* and *most ornamental.* Regard being had for the several Professions for which they are intended.

History was to be included but would be augmented by geography, the lives of great men, and contemporary history. Natural history—subjects that we would now call botany, physics, and chemistry—could be enriched by "*Gardening, Planting, Grafting, Inoculating,*" as well as by visits to successful farms where these methods might be observed. And most presciently, Franklin suggested courses such as "History of *Commerce,* of the Invention of Arts, Rise of Manufactures, Progress of Trade," in short, the types of subjects taught at the modern university. The University of Pennsylvania and its goals were strikingly foreshadowed by the institution that Franklin proposed.

Fearing that the new Academy and Charitable School could be readily converted to serve one denomination, Franklin selected an ecumenical board. Its members came from each of the major religions of the city and included Quakers, Baptists, and Presbyterians, as well as the Anglicans who might have been expected to strive for control. Most of the trustees had been engaged in city politics, and all but a few were members of the emerging wealthy class of merchants. A similar strategy led to his employing ministers of various churches as teachers including his friend and co-experimenter with electricity, Ebenezer Kennersley, who was also a Baptist minister.

Instead of erecting a new school building in the vicinity of the State House where it might have been turned to the goals of the ruling class,

*Fourth Street campus after original elevation by Pierre Eugène du Smitière, c. 1770*

Franklin acquired an existing structure that had been built for the congregation of charismatic preacher George Whitefield. Constructed in 1740 from
plans of carpenter Edmund Wooley, the architect of Independence Hall, it
was one of the largest buildings in the American colonies. Unlike traditional
Episcopal churches, which were oriented to place the altar on the east and
the entrance on the west, Whitefield's church ran north and south but probably placed its pulpit on the west side, denoting by its lack of orientation and
different form its independence from the English established church. In 1740
an interdenominational board, whose membership eventually included
Franklin, proclaimed the intention of serving the entire city by providing a
school for its children.

 Franklin and the new board purchased the Whitefield Chapel at a
time when its congregation was much diminished because of their minister's
continuing travels through the American colonies. As a result, the building
could be acquired at a fraction of its true value, solving two problems for
Franklin—the provision of meeting space for the new Academy and
Charitable School and the payment of the debt of the congregation on
whose board Franklin sat. Modifications were undertaken by a newcomer to
the city, master builder and architect Robert Smith, who had trained in
Scotland, presumably in the circle of Robert Adam. Smith added a belfry
housing a bell at one end to call students to classes, subdivided the lower
floor into rooms for the classrooms, and adapted the upper story to serve as

"the College Hall"—a great room that could house the entire school community as well as citizens of the city. The name of this room, College Hall, is now the title accorded to the central administrative building of the modern campus, which like its predecessor, contains a great auditorium on the second story.

With scientific apparatus purchased for its use, the Academy and Charitable School opened with a sermon whose theme anticipated the revolution to come: "And ye shall know the truth and the truth shall set you free." The new school drew from the entire continent; within four years, the student body rose from seventeen to more than 200. This led Franklin to initiate the second part of his plan—adding a college that would provide a more advanced education. For this enterprise Franklin selected Anglican-trained Scotsman William Smith to serve as provost, based on the latter's advocacy of a broad curriculum similar to the one that Franklin had proposed five years before.

In 1762, Provost Smith went to England in search of donations for a new dormitory building. This was also intended to contain classrooms for the Charitable School so that the school could be separated from the academy and collegiate classes that remained in the original building. The New College, as the building was called, was also designed by Robert Smith, this time in high Georgian design characterized by absolute symmetry and the diminishing stories of post–Renaissance classicism. Its conventional English style denoted the increasingly narrow religious background of the school, which under Provost Smith turned in the direction of an Anglican seminary to meet the requirements of the donors for the new building. With Smith as leader, Franklin was forced from the board of the College, Academy and Charitable School of Philadelphia. For the next generation, he watched from a distance while his creation struggled.

Smith's new classical curriculum caused the preparatory Latin school and the college to languish while the English and the mathematical lower schools continued to flourish. In the college, the sciences were reduced and might have disappeared altogether had it not been for the fortuitous addition in 1765 of a program in medicine where the modern sciences continued to be taught. Tapping the desire for professional training, the medical school quickly rivaled and then exceeded the college in size, attracting students from North and South America as well as from England and Ireland.

The growth of the medical school necessitated the construction of a Surgeon's Hall at Fifth Street, midway between the college and Pennsylvania Hospital where many of the faculty practiced. A surgical amphitheater was located on its upper level under a glazed cupola where students could see operations performed. The lower level housed the first laboratories in chemistry and botany. Just before the Revolution, one last building was constructed on the original campus—a home for Provost

*William Russell Birch,* Library and Surgeons Hall, in Fifth Street, Philadelphia; *Plate 13 from* The City of Philadelphia . . . as it appeared in the Year 1800

Smith. It stood at the corner of Fourth and Arch streets, and like all of the original campus, was demolished in the nineteenth century. The site of the first campus is now occupied by a Holiday Inn. Mounted plaques commemorate the early history of the institution.

      William Penn's policy of religious freedom made Philadelphia the site where the Continental Congresses debated the colonial response to British policy and in 1776 chose political independence. In Philadelphia alone there were the churches, chapels, meetings, and synagogues that could serve members of the many denominations who had come to the American colonies for religious freedom. While the city was the seat of the Congress, the college continued in much reduced circumstances with many of its students serving in the army. During the year of 1777, when the British occupied the city, the college was closely allied with the city's Tory leaders. When the patriots returned in 1779, they dismantled the board and reestablished the school under the new name of the University of the State of Pennsylvania. Its board once again included secular leaders as well as ministers from all of the denominations of the city, and its name reflected its multiple schools. The University of the State of Pennsylvania was the first to take this lofty title in the new American nation.

      After the Revolution, Provost Smith returned from exile in Maryland to reclaim his position at the college. When his claims were

*William Russell Birch,* The House intended for the President of the United States, in Ninth Street Philadelphia, *Plate 19 from* The City of Philadelphia . . . as it appeared in the Year 1800

accepted by the legislature, the university was forced to rent rooms from the American Philosophical Society. The result was a diminishing of support for each institution, which was resolved in 1791 by merging them into the University of Pennsylvania. Thus, the present university owes its origins to the University of the State of Pennsylvania, established by the Revolutionary councils of Philadelphia in 1779; the Academy and Charitable School founded by Franklin in 1749; and, by the broadest definition, to the school that was intended to be founded in Whitefield's chapel in 1740.

*Penn's Second Campus*

As the century of the Revolution ended, the original campus was cramped and problems developed because many students were not paying their dormitory bills. In 1800 after the federal government had departed for Washington, D.C., the mansion built as a home for the President of the United States was deemed surplus and put up for sale. Constructed as a gift of the people of Pennsylvania, it had never served its original purpose due to the provision of the Constitution that the president should receive his salary and "no other Emolument from the United States or any of them." The

*Ninth Street campus, J. C. Wild,* University of Pennsylvania, Philadelphia, *Plate 15 of Wild and Chevalier,* Views of Philadelphia, and its Vicinity, *1838*

house was designed by William Williams, the son-in-law of the late Robert Smith, in the manner initiated by British architect Robert Adam. Adams's new mode based on his discoveries in Herculanaeum established the style of the new nation and was used on the President's House. Embellished with elongated pilasters and a richly carved cornice, capped by a massive balustrade and a crowning dome above a central stair, it was far larger and more ornamental than any individual house in the city. In 1800 when the state and federal governments departed from the city, there were few uses for such a structure.

The house was advantageously located on an entire city block that spanned from Market Street on the north to Chestnut Street on the south between Ninth and Tenth streets. This afforded space for the institution to grow while the building could house the Academy and Charitable School on the ground floor and the College on the upper levels, replicating spatially the hierarchy of the institution. Benjamin Latrobe (1764–1820), a British-trained architect then working on the city's new waterworks, made the plans that adapted the building to its new purposes. He abandoned the upper story, however, thus forcing the Medical School to retain its classrooms in the Surgeons' Hall.

Latrobe returned to the campus in 1810 to design the medical hall that was attached to the south facade of the President's House. Here, Latrobe departed from Williams's overlay of Adam-based detail for a more original approach that used volume and fenestration to describe the internal functions. Seven years later, Latrobe's student William Strickland (1788–1854) enlarged the seating capacity—reflecting the continued expansion of the Medical School and the success of classes by Philadelphia's premier scientist of the day, chemist Robert Hare. That growth persisted into the 1820s, eventually forcing the trustees to consider a new building for the Medical School, which Strickland proposed to build on the south portion of the campus.

When the College learned that it was being left behind in the old building, it too petitioned for new quarters. Thus, a pair of buildings was constructed whose facades were ornamented with the pilasters and capitals removed from the President's mansion. Surfaced in yellow stucco, which was ruled and jointed to look like large blocks of stone, they continued the simple design of the early republic long after Strickland had adapted the Greek revival style for federal and civic buildings in the city. These buildings housed the university until after the Civil War, when new courses were initiated under a new Board of Trustees drawn from the industries of the city and a new provost who aimed to return to the vision of Franklin.

### Provost Stillé's West Philadelphia Campus

The third campus of the University of Pennsylvania resulted from the vision of English Professor and Provost Charles Stillé (1819–1899)—the first secular leader of the institution since Franklin more than a century before. Like Franklin, Stillé foresaw the potential of the institution to meet the needs of contemporary society. Drawing on Matthew Arnold's *Schools and Universities on the Continent* (1868), Stillé called for a new curriculum that would meet the needs of the rapidly industrializing city:

> . . . it cannot be disguised any longer that it is *the modern spirit*, especially in the form in which it has been developed in this country, which is now the open enemy of the old system of college education. . . . We are told by Mr. Matthew Arnold . . . there spreads a growing disbelief in Latin and Greek and a growing disposition to make modern languages and natural sciences take their place.

Putting these thoughts into action, Stillé proposed that a new campus be constructed in West Philadelphia. This would house the enlarged scientific department that had been funded before the Civil War but only partially realized. Watching the city's rapid growth and transformation—new buildings were under construction everywhere, and the railroad changed the city's overall appearance—Stillé decided to hire a professor of architecture who would teach courses in drafting and design while also helping determine whether the existing buildings of the campus could meet the needs of the future.

*G. M. Hopkins,* Atlas of West Philadelphia *(Philadelphia 1872), Detail of Plate B.*

The position was filled by Thomas Webb Richards (1836–1911), who had attended the Franklin Institute's course in architecture and during the Civil War had served as a hospital designer. Richards agreed to establish a course in architecture, the nation's second after the course established at the Massachusetts Institute of Technology. Simultaneously, he undertook a survey of the Strickland buildings, which he reported were unsuited for their growing task. With this ammunition, Stillé urged his board to acquire a new site for a new campus.

Fortunately, Stillé's new board was ready for the task. Unlike previous boards, which were dominated by ministers from the city's churches, the post–Civil War board included machine tool maker and President of the Franklin Institute William Sellers and merchant John Welsh who had important connections with the federal government. Under their leadership, the university negotiated the acquisition of land across the Schuylkill River at the rear of the immense property used by the city for its poorhouse and public hospital. The new property fronted on Woodland Avenue, a principal diagonal from the Market Street Bridge, with the promise of additional space if future growth required it. Stillé plunged ahead of his board, asking Richards to make studies of possible schemes for the new buildings. This action would have been appropriate in the coming generation when college presidents would lead their institutions with advice from their boards, but that moment was yet to come. The board asserted its control by withdrawing

*34th Street Campus, looking southeast after 1878*

the commission from Richards and sponsoring a competition open to all of the architects of the city. This occurred at the moment when a local chapter of the American Institute of Architects was founded, whose goals precluded architects undercutting each other. As a consequence, few of the city's leading designers submitted projects, leaving Richards the victor for the design of College Hall.

Richards envisioned College Hall as the first building of a complex that would be unified by siting and style. His design followed the so-called academic Gothic, the most notable examples being William Butterfield's polychromed Keble College at Oxford and William Burges's buildings at Hartford's Trinity College. Where Butterfield used red brick as the principal material, Richards selected a West Chester serpentine—a brilliant green local stone then much esteemed by Victorian designers who sought to contrast with the monochromes of pre–Civil War design. Accented with a silvery-gray schist, purple and yellow sandstones, and with multicolored slates on the roofs and towers, College Hall looked to the English colleges for its detail just as Stillé had relied on Matthew Arnold when he began thinking about a new curriculum. The new building initiated the celebration of student life that would characterize American colleges after the Civil War as sports and other affiliated activities were grafted to the lectures and classes of early colleges. At Penn, the red and blue slates in the roof and inlaid on the porch marked the selection of the collegiate colors that future Penn athletes would wear in competition.

Over the next few years, Richards designed the second and third buildings of the campus: the new Medical School (now Logan Hall), which faced 36th Street to the south and the rear of College Hall, and the new Hospital of the University of Pennsylvania, which was placed on the south side of Spruce Street. Each shared the palette of materials of the campus, though without the towers and articulated wings that enlivened College Hall and indicated its central role. In 1878, Richards completed the fourth building of the campus, the Robert Hare Laboratory, where Williams Hall now stands. Named for the great scientist who taught chemistry in the Medical School for nearly half a century, it also was of green serpentine with polychromatic Gothic detail. Its roof was crowned with an array of ventilation stacks denoting its function as a laboratory. The Hare Laboratory marked the shift in medical education away from lecture and toward hands-on training and research.

With the completion of the Hare Laboratory, the final form of Stillé's campus could be seen. The arts and sciences divisions of the college, the central administration, and the library were located in College Hall, which stood at the center of the institution. Medicine, though relegated to the side and rear, once again comprised the largest part of the university. There was room to the east for additional buildings that could serve the rapidly growing undergraduate population. The new campus attested to Stillé's vision, but he was still limited by his board. When a conflict developed over the disciplining of a student whose father sat on the board, Stillé was forced to resign after twelve years of leadership. Ironically, the present campus contains no memorial to the Moses who led his university into the future.

*William Pepper, M. D.: The Poetry of the Present*

Stillé was replaced by Dr. William Pepper (1843–1898; 1862, M.D. 1864) who as a trustee in the 1870s had directed the planning of the hospital and ensured that research laboratories were part of its plan. Pepper brought an originality of thought and an active involvement in contemporary science that transformed the academic life of the university. Under Pepper, thirteen departments and programs were established, including the Department of Finance and Economy (the Wharton School) in 1881, the Departments of Philosophy (the Graduate School) in 1883, Veterinary Medicine (1882), Biology (1883), Physical Education (1883), Nursing (1888), Archaeology and Paleontology (1889), Hygiene (Public Health, 1891), and Women (1891). Architecture was enlarged from the original program and given its separate professor in 1891.

These changes were reflected in the physical appearance of the university, which expanded south across Spruce Street and later to the east side of 34th Street and the west side of 36th Street. The resulting buildings followed the model of the Stillé campus setting individual structures for separate departments amidst open lawns. Location was determined by proximity

LEFT: *Frederick Gutekunst,* Hospital of the University of Pennsylvania, *c. 1885*
RIGHT: The Buildings and Property, of the University of Pennsylvania *from* Catalog and Announcements of the University of Pennsylvania, 1885–1886

to related structures, creating distinct precincts that still determine the present campus. The Medical School, the Hare Building, and the hospital were located south and west of College Hall. Future medical facilities were sited below the diagonal of Woodland Avenue and west of the college. In contrast to Richards's academic Gothic designs of serpentine stone, the new campus buildings were constructed of brick—taking on the image of the industrial culture that was shaping contemporary Philadelphia.

The first of the new buildings, near the hospital, housed the Biology Department in a bristling brick design that looked like an industrial laboratory. The next building on the west side of the campus housed the new School of Veterinary Medicine. It was designed by Frank Furness (1839–1912) in an assemblage of forms and materials that might have been jarring in the colleges of historicizing New England but were customary in industrial Philadelphia.

At Penn and elsewhere, courses usually took the form of lectures from faculty followed by recitations by students to ensure that time-tested material was passed on to a new generation. Provost Pepper was at home in the culture of scientific research that advanced the cause of "new knowledge." New knowledge was attained in the laboratory and by careful research in the library. Heretofore, a single room in College Hall had served as the library, but the new research methods required a new building. In 1886, Provost Pepper called for the erection of the best college library in America to meet the changing nature of education. Instead of relying on historic building models, the university assembled a committee that included architect Frank Furness, library consultant Melvil Dewey, and Harvard Chief Librarian Justin Winsor to devise a basic scheme for the new building.

Furness's plan merged the insights of the library experts with the evolving production-based architecture of regional industry. The library was planned with two principal points of entrance, one for the general user facing the campus, and the other facing 34th Street for the staff and deliveries. From the street entrance, books were brought into the cataloguing department, numbered, catalogued, and then delivered to the book stack. Users entered a spacious stair tower that provided access to an auditorium at the top of the stairs and to the main room of the library. Directly opposite the doors was the card catalog, the new tool for finding books. Adjacent to it was the main desk where books could be ordered from the book storage area. At the opposite end of the library was the main reading room, which in turn was surrounded by a ring of small seminar rooms, one for each academic department. Here, faculty could teach small classes surrounded by the principal books of their program.

The building shared with the factories and the giant machines manufactured in Philadelphia a revolutionary approach that generated design from the facts of the problem. University trustee and machine tool maker William Sellers claimed, "If a machine is right it looks right." Penn's library followed this progressive model. The book storage area was one of the most remarkable features: It was constructed of steel with a glass floor and roof that was designed to avoid the need for gas lighting, which could harm wood pulp–based paper of modern publishing. Moreover, it was designed to accommodate future expansion to the south as the collection increased. Like the self-adjusting machines manufactured in Philadelphia, it could be adapted to future needs.

As the library was being finished, the last remaining corner site of the main campus—where Irvine Auditorium now stands—was given to a power plant and engineering building. The architects were the Wilson Brothers, who had independently arrived at the methods of wind-braced, curtain-wall, steel-frame high-rise construction in the 1870s. They operated a national practice that designed elevated trains in New York, foundries in Colorado, and railroad bridges throughout the nation. Their power plant was crowned by a raised ventilating roof to cool the giant dynamo and a towering chimney, the typical landmark of industrial Philadelphia. Adjacent was a new building for the Engineering School, which looked like the office of a factory complex. The red brick library with its foundry-like book stack and the adjacent power plant and Engineering School marked Penn's shift from the remembered forms of the academic Gothic to the energy and power of the industrial architecture that typified contemporary Philadelphia.

As the nineteenth century ended, more than two-thirds of Penn's students took courses in engineering and the sciences, while medicine continued to be the university's largest single program. And, unlike Penn's peers to the north and south that were still controlled by boards largely made up of ministers of the founding denominations, Penn's board was composed almost entirely of industrialists, scientists, medical doctors, and lawyers. The programs that grew under Pepper's leadership and characterized his university reflected the goals and limitations of the city's industrial culture. Philadelphians had a profound mistrust of finance and based their fundraising for the expanding university on the growth of the region's industry. When those industries prospered, they provided regular support—but little that could be spared to build an endowment. In the Great Depression of the 1930s and again after World War II as industries failed, Philadelphia and its university suffered from their dependence on industry.

In other important aspects, however, Pepper turned toward the present. In 1890 the city's chapter of the American Institute of Architects asked for permission to take over the architecture program, which had ossified under Victorian Thomas Richards. After a year under the Philadelphia architect Theophilus Parsons Chandler, who worked most closely from historical models, Ecole des Beaux Arts–trained Warren P. Laird (1851–1948) was asked to head an enriched and enlarged program. His faculty drew on the new generation of architects led by Wilson Eyre, Jr.; Walter Cope; John Stewardson; and Frank Miles Day, who together transformed the city and the university. Similar cosmic shifts occurred across the entire institution under Pepper. Women, who had been permitted to take classes in limited departments as early as 1875, were incorporated into the university on a large scale with the creation of the Department for Women, the ancestor of the Education Department. During his years as provost, Pepper doubled the size and transformed the potential of his university into an engine of innovation.

### *Romantic Vision: The Campus of Provost Charles C. Harrison*

Though Charles Harrison (1844–1929; 1862) had graduated from the college in the same class as William Pepper, his work experience as a manufacturer of sugar pointed him away from the scientific and engineering values of Pepper and toward the rising consumer culture with its new arts of retailing and advertising. Harrison saw that vast projects aimed at the city would help him raise funds that were needed to meet the expanding mission of the university. Relying on personal contacts, Harrison pursued the old families, the traditional source of support of the university, as well as the new money centered along North Broad Street. The first building of the Harrison era was the University Museum. Instead of hiring Frank Furness (who had designed Harrison's own house and office), Harrison commissioned the junior faculty of Laird's architecture program, Wilson Eyre, Jr.; Frank Miles Day; Walter Cope; and John Stewardson, to work together on the project.

If Harrison's aim was to force each architect out of his accustomed modes to achieve a building that would represent the nontraditional anthropological collection of objects, then he succeeded beyond his wildest dreams. Two schemes were presented that reflected the battle of the styles of the day. One was a classical design loosely based on the Pantheon that joined gable-roofed buildings with domed buildings at the rear. The preferred scheme was a lyrical and whimsical fusion of historic forms based on the North Italian Romanesque with hints of the orient in the overlay of decorative tile ornaments. The brick field linked the design to the Victorian campus. Anticipating the free style of the Arts and Crafts, the design also managed to represent the multiple cultures displayed inside.

With the museum under construction, Harrison next moved to solve the campus's lack of student amenities. Though Penn attracted students for academic training, it had yet to develop the zest of student activities that was beginning to characterize contemporary colleges. To correct this failing, Harrison undertook three symbolically charged building projects, beginning with a competition among Penn's architecture students to design the nation's first student union on the English model. This again led to the question of the appropriate style for the building. A national jury including Laird; William Rutherford Mead of McKim, Mead and White; and others favored a design based on the English late-Gothic–styled Peacock Inn at Rowley, Yorkshire. Organized around a great hall containing a monumental stair with great fireplaces at each end, Houston Hall held dining and game rooms, as well as a swimming pool in the basement, all wrapped in medieval detail—the epitome of the undergraduate idea of a men's club. Harrison later delighted in recalling the effect of Houston Hall on President Eliot of Harvard. "President Eliot was in Philadelphia and I had the delight of showing him the unusual opportunities of student life afforded by Houston Hall. Mr. Eliot was more than interested and after a brief period following his departure for Boston, I heard that Mr. Eliot had secured a similar addition to the facilities of Harvard which is known as the Harvard Union."

Harrison then turned to the construction of a dormitory that would return Penn to a residential campus for the first time since its departure from the Arch Street site in 1801. For that building and most future projects until his retirement in 1910, he selected the architectural firm of Walter Cope and John Stewardson. Cope (1860–1902) had trained with the architect of Quaker Philadelphia, Addison Hutton, while Stewardson (1858–1896) had been a veteran of Frank Furness's office before they worked together in the office of beaux-arts–trained Theophilus Parsons Chandler. Together, they were the principal practitioners of the historically accurate collegiate Gothic, which they spread across the country with buildings at Princeton, Bryn Mawr, the University of Missouri at Columbia, and at Washington University in St. Louis. Under Harrison, Penn's buildings would be based on the English Gothic of the sort that characterized the colleges at Oxford and Cambridge so that all who saw the campus would know of its allegiances as

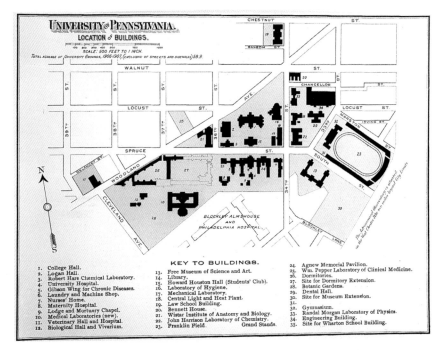

The University of Pennsylvania. Location of Buildings *from* Catalog and Announcements of the University of Pennsylvania, 1906–1907

well as its standing. Using this style, Penn joined new institutions such as the University of Chicago, historic universities that were moving to new sites such as Columbia, and old institutions such as Princeton, Yale, and Harvard, in choosing historic styles to represent their future.

The "Quad," as the dormitory quadrangles have always been called, marked Harrison's vision of the enlarging scale of the institution. It also stressed the importance of connecting to the national theme of historically based collegiate design rather than the region's industrially based cultural independence of the Pepper era. Its red brick and limestone colors and late-Gothic detail were based on St. John's College, Cambridge, which John Stewardson visited in 1895. His watercolor rendering of the brick "Backs of St. John's College," glowing red along the streamside, persuaded the university to shift from the gray stone that had been used at Houston Hall to the urban brick that continued the hue of the Pepper campus.

A third building aimed at student life was Franklin Field, which Harrison conceived as a link to the broader community. Its construction marked the shift of the athletic campus to the east side along the Schuylkill and presented a populist image of the university to the city. Harrison also hired the Yale coach George Woodruff and stocked the university with football talent, including John Heisman in the Law School and John Outland in the college. Over the next generation as Penn's football program grew,

Franklin Field was expanded to house vast crowds. The lower level of the present stadium was built in 1922 and the steel-framed upper deck was added two years later, bringing the capacity to 70,000.

In addition, Harrison undertook the fund-raising that brought the Law School west from its site on Independence Square. Its new building adhered to the color scheme of Cope and Stewardson's campus but stylistically, it was derived from the English baroque of Wren's Hampton Court to represent the English baroque origins of the American legal system. The Law School was followed by four immense classroom and laboratory buildings: the Towne Building, which served the Engineering School; the John Morgan Medical Laboratory for the Medical School; the Veterinary School; and Leidy Hall, which replaced the Biology Department. Together, these buildings doubled the compact campus of Provost Pepper, expanding it along the diagonal of Woodland Avenue from 33rd Street to 39th Street.

When Harrison retired in 1910, his successor, Professor of Chemistry Edgar Fahs Smith, turned to a committee to develop a plan for campus growth. It was headed by Fine Arts Dean Warren Laird and his professor of design, the French-born and Ecole des Beaux Arts–trained Paul Phillipe Cret (1876–1945), along with the Olmsted Brothers. Their introductory text dealt with the problem of scale of the modern university. It concluded that the Victorian manner of isolated buildings framed by lawns should be replaced by a new system of large buildings along street fronts that framed interior space. The dormitory group and the laboratory buildings by Cope and Stewardson had already made the shift to linear groupings that surrounded and shaped interior courts and lawns, but the Cret plan intended to extend the system in a series of spatially organized precincts across the entire university.

Even as Penn's campus planning was being rationalized, a group of alumni who perhaps too literally sought to compete with such peer institutions as Princeton, Dartmouth, and Yale proposed to strengthen the undergraduate college by removing it from the pressures and temptations of the city to a more remote location. There it could be housed in small dormitories that would create close and lasting personal bonds between students and faculty. The programs for women and the graduate school were to remain in the city. In 1929, the university accepted a large tract of land at Valley Forge, and plans were begun to move the College to its fourth location in a colonial revival campus. Fortunately, the immense costs slowed the process until the Depression, and World War II ended all such possibilities for a generation.

The Depression caused massive changes across the university. Instead of developing an independent endowment, the university had depended on the great industries of the region for support. When those industries slowed and their annual support was reduced, Penn was forced to cut programs and reduce expenditures on building. To fill vacancies, women

ENIAC, *1946*

were admitted to more and more graduate programs though they were still excluded from most undergraduate classes, as well as from most of the male-dominated organizations such as Houston Hall. World War II further shifted the student mix to include large numbers of women, but not until the 1960s, would women be treated as fully equal members of the university.

*Building a Future: The Presidencies of Harold Stassen and Gaylord P. Harnwell*

The late 1940s brought a flood of new and returning students, many of whom were veterans who could take advantage of the GI Bill. Based on the wartime success of federal research programs such as the development of the first electronic computer, ENIAC, at Penn's Moore School in 1946, federal programs provided research support and construction money for new facilities. Simultaneously, federal urban redevelopment programs made it possible to envision institutional expansion on a vast scale. Philadelphia was in the nation's spotlight for its energetic urban reform under City Planner Edmund Bacon, and for its position as host city for all three political party conventions in 1948. When the Republican Party turned from Harold Stassen to Thomas Dewey, the university trustees selected Stassen (1907–2001) as its next president in the hope that he would help return the

OPPOSITE: *Jacob Stelman*, Aerial view of campus, *1940*

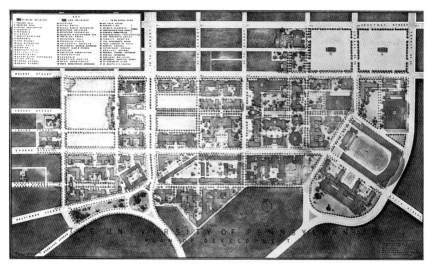

*Grant Simon, Executive Architect,* The University of Pennsylvania,
Plan of Development, *1948*

university to national prominence while setting the stage for a later campaign for the presidency.

The first non-Philadelphian to lead the university since William
Smith, Stassen, the former "boy-wonder" governor of Minnesota, was accustomed to executive action and quickly began the process of transforming the
university. During his four years as president, Stassen deemphasized football,
making it possible for Penn to join the new Ivy League athletic conference. He
also began a push for academic excellence by bringing in new leadership to
head university departments. One of Stassen's most important acts was to
replace George Koyl (Arch. 1911), the aging beaux-arts–trained dean of the
School of Fine Arts, with G. Holmes Perkins (1904– ). Perkins, a Harvard-
trained architect and planner who had studied under Walter Gropius, was a
strong advocate of modern design. Under Perkins, the School of Fine Arts was
reshaped into a powerful force for innovation with faculty members including
urban historian Lewis Mumford; ecologist Ian McHarg; and architects Louis
I. Kahn, Romaldo Giurgola, Robert Venturi, and Denise Scott Brown. As
Laird had guided Provost Harrison, Perkins guided Stassen, heading the campus design committees and playing a major role in selecting the architects who
would shape Penn's expansion.

In 1948, even before Perkins's arrival, Penn's leaders asked a
group of its senior architecture graduates headed by Grant Simon (Arch.
1911) and Sydney Martin (1908) to devise a new plan for the campus.
Their plan reflected their beaux-arts training. This is particularly obvious in their proposal to remove all of the hated Victorian buildings

OPPOSITE: *Grant Simon, Executive Architect,* The University of Pennsylvania,
Plan of Development, *1948*

including Logan Hall and Frank Furness's library. In their place, bland moderne classical buildings of four and five stories would be constructed continuing the color scheme of the Harrison campus but lacking its historicizing detail. Fortunately for the present campus, those decisions were delayed, permitting the later restoration of some of the most vital parts of the modern campus. But the planners' vision of removing streets to create oversized blocks of campus and their general goal to extend the campus west along a pedestrian spine on the former Locust Street have proven successful.

Before the arrival of Perkins, the donors or the Board of Trustees selected architects from a limited group who designed their houses and businesses. The new process was led by the dean with one guideline from the trustees—that architects had to have graduated from the university or be on its faculty. Perkins added another requirement—that modern principles guide design. Penn's next president, Gaylord P. Harnwell (1903–1982), came from the science faculty and was comfortable with modern design. As the Cold War intensified, federal aid became available to fund university expansion, particularly in the sciences and graduate studies. The first needs to be met were for a cluster of modern laboratories that were added to the old science precinct on the east and to the medical research center on the west. These buildings announced new design currents that eventually would erode the principles of Euro-modernism as developed by Walter Gropius and Ludwig Mies van der Rohe. Instead, they helped establish the maxims of the so-called Philadelphia School that grew around the teaching and practice of Penn's new design professor, Louis Kahn (1901–1974, Arch. 1924). The first to be completed was Robert Geddes's elegant infill Pender Laboratory between the Towne and Moore schools. It utilized a prefabricated, reinforced concrete frame flanked by panels of Flemish bond brick, which provided a contextual link to the adjacent buildings.

Kahn's Alfred Newton Richards Medical Research Building broke out of the glass box and universal space paradigms of the International School, returning to the functional expression and formal articulation that had characterized Frank Furness's work in Philadelphia and had been continued by other American modernists including Frank Lloyd Wright and George Howe. Perhaps not coincidentally, Kahn's architectural studio met in the upper lecture hall of the old University Library, and he had worked with Howe in the 1930s. In any event, Kahn's laboratory was a revelation and was hailed by Wilder Green in his text for a Museum of Modern Art exhibit brochure as "the most consequential building since the war." Green described Kahn as having "an ethical sense of purpose strong enough to control and qualify pure aesthetic invention, and equaled by no other architect in this country." These qualities affected much of Penn's campus in the 1960s.

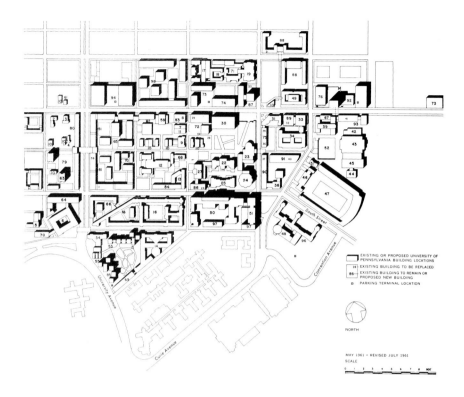

Campus Development Plan, *1961*

Other buildings represented the incipient revolution away from the minimalist mode of international modern. Eero Saarinen's contextual design for Hill House (now Hill College House) surrounded a roofed-over interior court with the blocky massing of Philadelphia rowhouses, colored by the red clinker brick of industry and the old library and capped by a metal comb-like cornice. (Though Saarinen had not attended Penn and was not teaching on its faculty, it was decided that having Penn graduates in his office qualified him for the commission.) Mitchell/Giurgola's garage at 33rd and Walnut streets explored Kahn's interest in structure as a generator of form, while their later Education Wing for the University Museum incorporated the brick details and tile roof in a carefully conceived contextual design. More recently, the Clinical Research Building on the medical campus and the Vagelos Laboratory at 34th Street, both by Venturi, Scott Brown and Associates, have continued the dialogue between place and purpose that characterizes the best of Penn's buildings.

Unfortunately, the projects funded by the state's General Services Administration were rarely as successful, but within Perkins's adaptable guidelines, Penn architecture was rarely constricted to a uniform architectural palette or one particular style. The result was a remarkable mixture that harmonized with the variety of the nineteenth-century campus while responding to the new requirements of the modern world. As Harnwell's tenure ended, he had once again doubled the size of the university while guaranteeing that it would stay in West Philadelphia and transforming it from a regional to a national university.

### The Campus of the Present

Titus Hewryk's foreword tells the story of the last generation from the vantage point of one of the shapers of the story. For our purpose in reaching the present campus, it is perhaps enough to mark one additional current—the incorporation of Penn's historic buildings into the future of the campus. If there was a chief limitation to modernism as practiced after World War II, it was the general hostility to context and history. No doubt this attitude was necessary to enable the modernists to force their way to the table—but once they were invited, it was as if rather than simply rearranging the seating plan, they threw out the furniture, rewrote the rules of etiquette, and demanded a new chef.

At Penn, the result was the demolition of many buildings of note to be replaced with contemporary buildings, often of lesser value. Thomas Richards's green serpentine Gothic Hare Laboratories was demolished for the undistinguished Williams Hall. Cope and Stewardson's elegant Italianate Harrison Chemistry Laboratory was replaced by the present Chemistry Building, and plans were made to demolish Furness's old University Library. Fortunately, in the case of the library, Frank Lloyd Wright visited the campus and recognized it as the work of the teacher of Louis Sullivan, his own master. Wright proclaimed the library to be "the work of an artist." With that endorsement, the library survived to be loved, admired, and finally restored.

As in physics, so too in art, for every action there is an equal and opposite reaction. As the 1970s ended, popular hostility to modernism produced the rise of the historic preservation movement. By the mid-1970s, the Quad was being updated with a New York loft look in the interior, but the exterior was being preserved if not restored. Under Presidents Sheldon Hackney and Judith Rodin (1966), Penn has balanced the need for new facilities with the care and restoration of many of its historic buildings, often under the direction of distinguished modern firms. Venturi, Scott Brown and Associates led the restoration and adaptive reuse of the old University Library, which removed the added floor that cut the great reading room atrium in half and returned the building to the forefront in the continuing reevaluation of Furness's work. More recently, Venturi, Scott Brown and Associates has undertaken the restoration of Houston Hall and the adaptive reuse of Irvine Auditorium to create a modern center for undergraduate life around the Perelman Quadrangle in the heart of the university.

Another recent initiative of the Rodin era has sought to revitalize the community around the university. The wealthy Victorian suburb into which Penn moved in the 1870s lost its allure in the early twentieth century as automobiles made the distant suburbs accessible. During World War II, many of its gracious houses were subdivided into apartments, and by the 1960s, many of the long-term residents left the neighborhood, fearing university expansion. The consequence was the rise of a transient student ghetto that was poorly served by the city and steadily deteriorated to the point that students and faculty began living across the Schuylkill. To meet this crisis, the university determined to build a permanent community by improving the region with first-class shopping facilities, providing incentives to buy and restore the historic houses of the neighborhood, and creating a university-supported community public school as a center of training for university students.

With these and other projects underway, Penn enters the twenty-first century in a wave of construction that now stretches from the Schuylkill River west beyond 40th Street and from Market Street on the north to Woodland Avenue on the south. The university has grown as it has faced the future and expanded its boundaries, both physical and mental. Again, these changes are reflected in its community and its Board of Trustees. Women are now equal participants in all aspects of university life. The principal degree awarded today is the Bachelor of Arts degree of the College, followed closely by the Bachelor of Science degree of the Wharton School of Business, and graduate degrees. The programs of the nineteenth century, engineering and medicine, follow. Not coincidentally, Penn's trustees are drawn from business and science, mirroring its successes in the last quarter of the twentieth century. Under President Rodin, the university is a rich amalgam of the peoples of the nation and of the globe who are welcomed to an institution that would make its founder proud.

*George E. Thomas, Philadelphia, PA*

A more detailed history with notes is available in George E. Thomas and David B. Brownlee, *Building America's First University: An Historical and Architectural Guide to the University of Pennsylvania.* (Philadelphia: University of Pennsylvania Press, 2000).

TOP: *Blanche Levy Park*
BOTTOM: *Main Campus*

## *Penn Treasures*

When Benjamin Franklin wrote of his plan for a modern education, he sagely noted of his students' studies that "Art is long, and their time is short." This led him to propose that their goal be to "learn those Things that are likely to be *most useful* and *most ornamental.*" With Franklin as our guide, and realizing that for many the first visit to Penn's campus requires haste, these highlights are intended as a taste that will lure the visitor back for longer and more extensive explorations by presenting the most original and most engaging campus sites. The text below can be augmented by additional material in the main guide portion of this volume.

Any tour of the campus should begin with two of the outdoor rooms of the campus: **Blanche Levy Park**, the front lawn of College Hall, and the Wynn Commons of the Perelman Quadrangle between College Hall and Houston Hall. Together these spaces form the central campus and contain the first buildings of Provost Stillé's renewed university. In the center of Levy Park is **College Hall**, the first building of the West Philadelphia campus. Built in 1870–1873 of a local brilliant green serpentine with polychromatic details in the Gothic style advocated by John Ruskin, College Hall is Thomas Richards's masterpiece and one of the chief Victorian buildings of the city. Its center block is flanked by distinct wings representing the division of the college into the faculties of the arts on the east and the sciences on the west, with the administration and library in the center. From the Gothic front portico, a restored entrance hall leads into an exhibit on the history of the university. The corridors are lined with portraits of Penn's leaders spanning its 250-plus years.

Directly east of College Hall is Frank Furness's old University Library, now called the **Fisher Fine Arts Library**. Furness taught Louis Sullivan, who in turn taught Frank Lloyd Wright—initiating one of the important lines of development toward modern architecture. Furness's fiery red brick, terra-cotta, tile, and sandstone contrast with the green Gothic College Hall. In the stair hall, Furness gives a lesson on the different states of iron—cast, wrought, and rolled—while the great skylighted reading room, restored by Venturi, Scott Brown and Associates, is an essay on the importance of natural light. Opening off the stair tower is the university's main changing exhibits space, the Arthur Ross Gallery, which occupies a room added in the 1930s to house the Shakespeare collection of Frank Furness's brother. In the basement entered off the stairs to 34th Street, is the Kroiz Gallery of the Architectural Archives, which contains drawings and models by Louis Kahn, Frank Furness, and other national luminaries of the profession.

The various spaces of the **main campus** are dotted with sculptures that reflect the evolution of modern art over the past century. In the center, in front of College Hall, is John J. Boyle's seated figure of *Benjamin Franklin* (1899), founder of the university. A favorite site for photographs, students also

*Houston Hall*

rub Franklin's foot for good luck. The shift toward abstraction is apparent in
Alexander Calder's *Jerusalem Stabile* (1979), which stands in front of Meyerson
Hall. It is one of the last works of a modern master whose father and grandfather's works ornament City Hall and the Swann Fountain of the Benjamin
Franklin Parkway. The return of subject matter transformed in scale and material was the subject of pop artists such as Claes Oldenberg, whose *Split Button*
(1981) in front of the Van Pelt Library illustrates at vast scale one of Poor
Richard's aphorisms. Robert Indiana's *Love* sculpture, adapted from his poster
of the same subject, has become an icon of the City of Brotherly Love.

   The second great space of the main campus is the **Wynn Commons**
of the Perelman Quadrangle, located between College Hall and Houston
Hall. Redesigned by Venturi, Scott Brown and Associates it links spaces
devoted to undergraduate life. It is dominated by Karl Bitter's seated bronze
figure of *Provost William Pepper* (1895). Across from College Hall is **Houston
Hall**, which was designed in a student competition to house the nation's first
student union (1894–1896) and set the university's course toward the historically accurate collegiate Gothic. Restored by the Venturi office, its great hall
is a center of information for current activities on campus; restaurants in the
basement offer a chance to experience the clamor of undergraduate life.
Scattered throughout the building are trophies of Penn's history, from the
College Hall bell to a handsome plaque dedicated to John Thayer, who was
on the fatal voyage of the HMS Titanic.

OPPOSITE: *William B. Irvine Auditorium*

Between the Fisher Fine Arts Library and Houston Hall stands **Irvine Auditorium**, Horace Trumbauer's towering homage (1926) to Mont St. Michel. Plagued by acoustical problems, it was long the subject of a student myth that it was a failed student project forced on the university by an angry parent. In fact, the poor acoustics were the result of too much interference by the client, but the building contains a stunning space made memorable by the psychedelic color of the Hollywood Gothic interior. Those features were preserved in a brilliant reformulation of the interior by Venturi, Scott Brown and Associates. They adapted the side seating areas to provide needed performance and café spaces while achieving an acoustically live hall that is now a regional showplace.

North of the main campus along Walnut Street is Penn's principal retail district. Its centerpiece is the Penn Bookstore at 36th Street, which fills the east end of the ground floor of the building of the Inn at Penn. Most of the necessities of campus life can be found in the two blocks of retail that begin at 34th Street. Half a block to the north, the restored Victorian townhouses of the 3400 block of Sansom Street offer a variety of intimate dining experiences.

*A Wider Loop*

If time permits, brief walks to the east and west offer additional Penn treasures. **Smith Walk** connects the central campus to the athletic precinct on the east and is headed by R. Tait McKenzie's seated figure of Professor of Chemistry and Provost Edgar Fahs Smith, who advised Edison on filaments for the light bulb and helped establish the field of electro-chemistry. Smith Walk is a quiet, old-fashioned design passing through the center of the School of Engineering and Applied Sciences. To the north on 33rd Street is the Moore School of Electrical Engineering, which contains a small museum on the construction of the world's first electronic computer, ENIAC—completed in 1946 by Penn scientists J. Prosper Eckert and John W. Mauchly.

Across 33rd Street are the buildings of the athletic campus fronting outdoor tennis courts. On the far side is **Penn's Palestra** (1926), the long-time home of Penn's basketball Quakers and Philadelphia's Big Five basketball rivalry. A gallery around its perimeter tells the story of the region's basketball history. To the south is the multistory arcade of **Franklin Field** (1922, upper deck 1925), the home of Penn football and the Penn Relays. South on 33rd Street is R. Tait McKenzie's *Young Franklin*, depicting the athletic vigor of the young man who arrived from Boston in 1722.

Across Spruce Street is the **University Museum** (1895 ff) designed by the young teachers of Penn's School of Architecture in a memorable synthesis of medieval and middle eastern styles with an arts and crafts flavor.

*Smith Walk*

The vaguely oriental entrance gate opens into the main entrance through the serene west courtyard. Within are some of the most remarkable treasures of the ancient Middle East, including the nearly 5000-year-old *Ram in a Thicket* from university excavations at Ur.

**Locust Walk** leads from the west side of the main campus to the university's Annenberg School of Communications and the Wharton School of Business and Finance. Locust Walk, created by closing Locust Street, is now the principal east-west axis of the university, linking the dormitories on the west with the academic center. As the main street of the campus, Locust Walk is the preferred location for student groups advertising performances and activities. It is at its most glorious on graduation day when Pennsylvania's red and blue colors are interspersed with the usual black academic robes. Along Locust Walk are several of the houses that once made fraternity row a male bastion. Most are now in general university use.

At 37th Street another seated sculpture of *Benjamin Franklin* by George W. Lunden (1987) marks one of the entrances to the Wharton campus and forms an appropriate spot for a photograph. In the distance are the towers of the dormitory Quadrangle and further south the modern towers of Louis Kahn's masterpiece, the Richards Medical Research Building. To the west, Locust Walk is elevated on a bridge over 38th Street toward the modern complex of high-rise apartments that house many of Penn's undergraduates.

## Central Campus

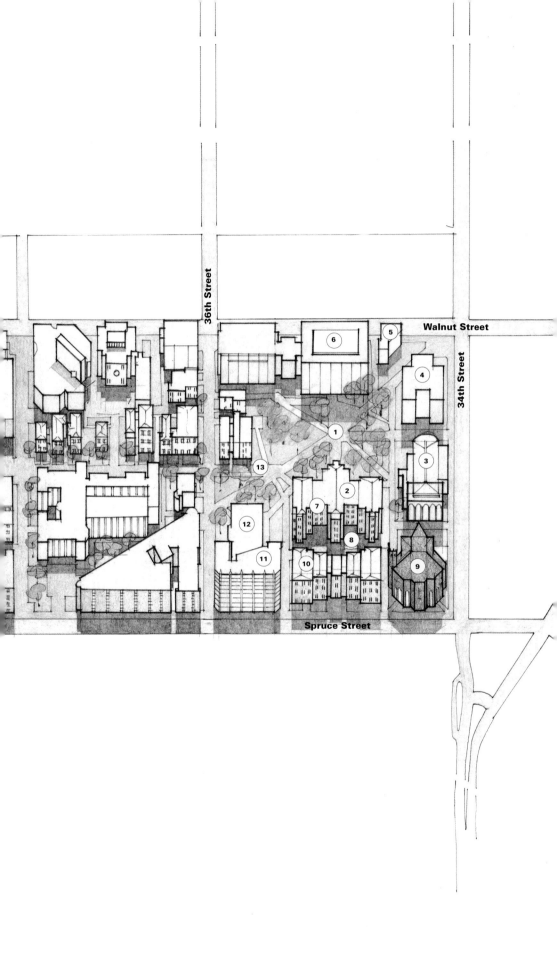

36th Street

Walnut Street

34th Street

Spruce Street

The Central Campus had its beginnings in 1870 when the trustees purchased a portion of the City Almshouse property between what are now Spruce, 34th, and 36th streets and Woodland Avenue, which once cut diagonally through the present campus green. Here, Provost Stillé envisioned a quadrangle of academic Gothic buildings that would serve the future needs of the university.

An early plan, probably by Richards, the university's professor of architecture, showed College Hall facing north toward Woodland Avenue with the Medical School and the new University Hospital directly to the south facing Spruce Street. While its size, ornamentation, and position would have established College Hall as the principal building of the new campus, the medical campus would have occupied the remainder of the available space, eliminating any prospects for growth and once again challenging the role of the college as the core of the institution. Fortunately, that plan was not followed. When the Medical School was built in 1874, it was turned deferentially to face 36th Street. The hospital—the first owned and operated by a university—was built on the south side of Spruce Street where it backed up to the existing buildings of the city's public hospital.

As the centerpiece of the new campus, College Hall was given a higher degree of elaboration. The future history of the campus would tell of the growth of departments and their removal one by one from College Hall.

In the 1880s university leaders sought to protect future expansion possibilities by judiciously siting new buildings to control unallocated city land. The first plans for the new University Library called for it to be built on the triangular property across from the Medical School, but when funding was obtained for an anatomical research laboratory, the Wistar Institute was built there, establishing that side of the campus as the medical precinct. Space along 34th Street provided sites for the new University Library and soon after for the power plant and Engineering School. None of these buildings took their cues from Richards's designs, responding instead to contemporary currents and establishing one of the future courses of the institution—the free interplay of modern designs in a historic setting. With the completion of the power plant and the library in 1891 and the construction of Houston Hall in 1895, the main campus was essentially filled. For later buildings the university was forced to look beyond its borders or to demolish obsolete structures (the power plant, for example, was replaced by Irvine Auditorium).

The Central Campus was nearly doubled in size in the 1960s, when the north half of the block between Walnut Street and Woodland Avenue was acquired as part of an urban renewal program. Beginning with the 1948 campus plan, this property had been viewed as the logical location for the next round of central university facilities, particularly a new central library. The construction of the Van Pelt Library reversed the trend of departmental libraries scattered around the campus and reinforced the central campus as a space shared by the entire university. At the beginning of the 1960s, the university hierarchy was obvious. The administration, the library, and the older liberal arts departments (particularly history and philosophy) were located on the core campus, their power reflected by proximity to the center. A symbolically significant battle erupted over the desire of the dean of the Graduate School of Fine Arts to place his school's new building on the main campus. Dean Perkins shoehorned the new fine arts building into a grove of elms that had long formed an important entrance to the campus, in the near vicinity of the old University Library (which had become the Fine Arts Library when the main collection was moved to Van Pelt). This was done over the objection of other departments, who viewed architecture and its related fields more as craft than intellectual discipline and thus unworthy of such prestigious space. In 1971 a much needed humanities classroom building, Williams Hall, was constructed on the site of the Hare Laboratory, beginning a pattern of growth by subtraction.

After the expansion of the 1960s and 1970s, the landscape of the central campus was in tatters. On the central campus, the roadbed of Woodland Avenue was removed, but the diagonals of street trees and sidewalks still cut through the block. Walks were little more than dirt paths across the patchy green. Trained as a landscape architect in his native Great Britain, the new dean of the Graduate School, Sir Peter Shepheard, persuaded the administration of the benefits of a comprehensive redesign for the central campus. Walks in a unifying palette of materials provided logical access to buildings while preserving areas for outdoor recreation. The landscape plan unified the central campus and in turn caused the university community to realize the value of its historic buildings. This led to the restoration and adaptive reuse of Furness's brilliant library, College Hall, and Logan Hall under President Hackney. More recently under President Rodin, Houston Hall and Irvine Auditorium have been restored as centerpieces of undergraduate life surrounding Perelman Quadrangle. As the twenty-first century begins, the Central Campus is the heart of the university.

*Blanche Levy Park*

## 1. Blanche Levy Park

*Sir Peter Shepheard, Laurie Olin, Andropogon Associates and others, 1977–1979*

The chief outdoor room of the university, Blanche Levy Park is the setting for College Hall and the main libraries. It is also the crossroads of the pedestrian system, making it the town square of the university. Its tree-shaded lawns divided by walks are dotted with sculptures that tell of the university history beginning with John J. Boyle's seated figure of the founder, *Benjamin Franklin* (1899), which originally stood in front of the federal building at 9th Street. Claes Oldenberg's *Split Button* (1981) illustrates an aphorism of Poor Richard, while David Lindquist's *Peace Symbol* (1970) recalls the conflict of the Vietnam War. Alexander Calder's bright red *Jerusalem Stabile* is located on the brick plaza between Frank Furness's Fisher Fine Arts Library and Meyerson Hall.

## 2. College Hall  *Thomas Webb Richards, 1870–1873*

Many American post–Civil War campuses followed the contemporary fashion of the Ruskinian Gothic, but Penn was probably unique in using serpentine as the building material for its principal buildings. In an age inflamed by Ruskin's *Lamp of Beauty*, serpentine was immensely popular in Philadelphia, being used on the Academy of Natural History, numerous

OPPOSITE: *College Hall*

churches, and Provost Stillé's own house near Rittenhouse Square. With accents of silvery gray schist and purple and yellow sandstones, columns of pink granite, and red and blue slates in the roof, Richards's design of College Hall was a celebration of the region's geology. Unfortunately, while serpentine survives in rural areas, it deteriorates rapidly in the pollution of the industrial city. By 1888, Penn had been forced to begin repairing the towers and walls of College Hall, and both towers were completely removed early in the twentieth century. Despite these losses, College Hall retains its Gothic vigor and color, in large measure due to a restoration of the exterior undertaken by restoration architect Marianna Thomas (Arch. 1972) and the Clio Group, Inc., beginning in 1988. The main entrance is through a Gothic porch facing the now removed Woodland Avenue. The wings housing the arts and science departments carried Gothic towers, one of which housed the college bell.

College Hall's north portico leads into a corridor that contains an exhibit on the university history and many of its chief administrative symbols, including the mace carried in academic processions. In the cross halls are portraits of Penn's leaders, including the first provost, William Smith, after the original by Gilbert Stuart. Because of its non-sectarian roots, Penn has never built a separate chapel, but Room 200 is lit by Gothic windows and serves that purpose. It contains other relics of the history of the university including the plaque for the John Welsh Professorship, and the Thomas Richards–designed plaque honoring the university sons who died in the Civil War. Within College Hall are offices of the president and provost, the admissions offices on the ground floor, the original assembly room of the college on the second story, and classrooms.

## 3. Fisher Fine Arts Library

*Frank Furness, of Furness, Evans, and Co., 1888–1891*

In 1886 Frank Furness joined with library expert, Melvil Dewey, and Chief Librarian of Harvard University, Justin Winsor, to meet Provost Pepper's charge to build the nation's best college library. Their discussion led away from historical forms to a fresh reformulation of library design that was planned to expedite the needs of the staff and the user. Most remarkable were their ideas for a "book stack," or storage system, that could be extended as the collection grew. The building reflects the utilitarian massing of the great factories of the region with the stair tower, chimney stack, and toilet facilities attached to the side of the main library volume rather than merged into it. Roof systems with ventilating window bands were borrowed

OPPOSITE: *Fisher Fine Arts Library*

*Fisher Fine Arts Library, reading room*

from foundry design, and the building was constructed of industrial red brick trimmed with red terra-cotta and red sandstone.

Internal design requirements, particularly an upper level auditorium that could be reached from the grand stair, caused the architect to round the north end of the building like the apse of a cathedral. Furness added gargoyles, providing an overlay of high architecture on the otherwise utilitarian design. Furness's original design for the leaded glass in the tympana over the entrance and scattered through the building brilliantly anticipates the curvilinear art nouveau and twentieth-century primitivism. Within, the multistory reading room is mosque-like in the cubic proportions of the

*Fisher Fine Arts Library*

space and the low canopy of table-mounted lights. Lighted overhead by a skylight that gathers every bit of available natural light for the reader, the reading room is one of the world's great Victorian spaces. Louis Kahn remembered the reading room of his college years when he designed the central void of the Exeter Academy Library.

In 1916 the Duhring Wing was added and the Lea Reading Room along 34th Street was added in 1923, both by Furness, Evans and Co. The moderne Gothic Horace Howard Furness Shakespeare Library on the front of the building was added in 1931 by Robert Rhodes McGoodwin (1907, Arch. 1912) as part of a scheme that would have clad the entire exterior in the style of Irvine Auditorium. Fortunately, the Depression stopped that project, making possible the 1986–1991 restoration and adaptive reuse by Venturi, Scott Brown and Associates with the Clio Group, Inc., and Marianna M. Thomas Architects. Venturi-designed tables and chairs emulate Furness's proportions and detail.

The library contains collections that serve the Graduate School of Fine Arts and Art History. Off the main entrance hall is the Arthur Ross Gallery, the university's changing exhibits venue; in the basement, entered off a landing at 34th Street, are the Kroiz Gallery and the Architectural Archives, which contain one of the premier collections of architectural drawings and models. At its center is the collection of Louis Kahn's papers, drawings, and models placed on permanent loan by the State of Pennsylvania.

*Meyerson Hall*

### 4. Meyerson Hall *Stewart, Noble, Class, and Partners, 1965–1968*

Named for former Professor of City Planning and University President
Martin Meyerson, Penn's fine arts building is one of a surprising number of
overwrought and generally unsuccessful design schools that dot the
nation's campuses. Its industrial skylights and concrete sunscreens crudely
mimic the meaning-filled designs of Louis Kahn, who was the luminary of
the Architecture School and the logical choice for its design. Instead of hiring Kahn, the school adapted an architectural thesis project that was turned
over to a firm with close connections to the university. The mean entrance
and contorted circulation of the building resulted from the last-minute adaptation of space that had been planned for the Institute for Contemporary Art
gallery to house faculty offices. The gallery was placed at the core of the
building, which had been intended as a gracious circulation space around a
grand stair to the basement court. With the removal of ICA to a separate
building (see North Campus), the central gallery is now used for student
exhibits and reviews, adding life to the interior.

*Elliot and Roslyn Jaffe History of Art Building*

## 5. Elliot and Roslyn Jaffe History of Art Building

*Oswin Shelly, 1900*

Designed by an alumnus of the Phi Delta Theta fraternity, the triangular shape and corner bay of the building were derived from the now-removed diagonal of Woodland Avenue. Shelly echoed the late English Gothic of the Quad and duplicated its rounded west end—a motif in turn mimicked by Zeta Psi across the intersection of 34th and Walnut streets. When the fraternity moved to larger quarters on Locust Street, the house was acquired by the university and eventually adapted to serve the needs of the History of Art Department by Tony Atkin (Arch. 1974) in 1990. His additions use the Flemish bond brick and limestone trim of the original but at the scale of the late twentieth century.

## 6. Charles Patterson Van Pelt Library

*Harbeson, Hough, Livingston, and Larson, 1960–1962*

The central research collection of the university, Van Pelt, is one of the world's premier academic libraries. Built in 1960 according to the intentions of the 1948 master plan, its giant concrete colonnade juxtaposes the beaux-arts classicism of Paul Cret's teaching and practice (here continued by his successor firm) against the modern conventions of asymmetry and building as volume. The result owes much to Eliel Saarinen's 1940s stripped classicism, but the small windows punctuating the upper levels denote readers' carrels in the

*Charles Patterson Van Pelt Library*

manner of Henri Labrouste's tiny windows in the Bibliothèque St. Genevieve. *The Family of Man* by Constantine Nivolo guards the entrance—another carry-over from beaux-arts practice where the integration of sculpture and building was an important part of the esthetic program. To the west, the same architects added the Dietrich Wing in 1965–1967, using similar materials but with a nod to Kahn's Richards Medical Research Building, which had been completed in the intervening years. The interior was given a slick cherry and chrome updating in 1998–1999 by Bower, Lewis, and Thrower Architects.

The sixth floor is devoted to special collections. It contains the walnut library designed circa 1880 by Collins and Autenreith for Henry Charles Lea's Walnut Street home. It was reinstalled in Furness, Evans and Co.'s addition to the old University Library in the 1920s and moved to Van Pelt in 1963. Across the corridor are the furnishings and fittings of Horace Howard Furness's Shakespeare Library that were originally installed in the room that Robert McGoodwin added to the front of the old library in the 1930s. In a first-floor lounge is a trophy of early university history, David Rittenhouse's *Orrery*, a clockwork model of the solar system. Its Chippendale-style case by Parnell Gibbs and John Folwell is one of the masterpieces of eighteenth-century Philadelphia cabinetry.

*Perelman Quadrangle*

### 7. Perelman Quadrangle *Venturi, Scott Brown and Associates, 1995–2000*

In the 1980s, changing undergraduate interests and the de facto shift of
Houston Hall to house administrative offices led to the development of
plans for a new student center across Walnut Street where the bookstore
and the Inn at Penn now stand. Fortunately, delays led to the decision to
restore Houston Hall, the nation's first student union, as the centerpiece of
the Perelman Quadrangle. Drawing on the planning skills of Denise Scott
Brown, spaces for a host of student facilities were found in the buildings
that surrounded the plaza between College Hall and Houston Hall. Gallery
space was created in the basement of Logan Hall, a brilliantly hued twenty-
four-hour-a-day study center was inserted in the dingy courtyard of
Williams Hall, and new performance spaces were captured in Irvine
Auditorium. The resulting complex restores undergraduate activity to the
heart of the campus.

### 8. Wynn Commons *Venturi, Scott Brown and Associates, 1998–2000*

To make the Perelman Quadrangle work it was necessary to provide space
for student meetings, organizations, and clubs, as well as restaurants and
study spaces, while at the same time adding service spaces such as
kitchens that could serve the food court in the basement of Houston Hall.
This was accomplished by excavating the space between College Hall and
Houston Hall and then roofing it with the plaza that is now a splendid

*Wynn Commons*

outdoor room. A rostrum backed by a pop version of Penn's insignia on the east and a bank of steps that serve as seats at the west end provide settings for outdoor activities. Limestone and enameled metal panels inscribed with significant events in the university history frame the principal entrances. At the center of the plaza at the rear of College Hall is Karl Bitter's seated portrait of *Provost William Pepper* (1895), who managed to continue his medical practice while serving on many of the city's boards and leading the university to greatness as a center of research activity. In this moving sculpture, Pepper is depicted in a moment of contemplation, raising his hand perhaps to initiate one of the numerous programs and departments listed on the bronze panel on the back.

### 9. William B. Irvine Auditorium  *Horace Trumbauer, 1926–1932*

Thanks in no small part to Henry Adams's published tribute, Mont St. Michel became the iconic Gothic building of the 1920s, encouraging Horace Trumbauer's homage to its exterior form as the envelope for an auditorium. Its ecclesiastical flavor compensated for Penn's unbuilt chapel, but its brilliant stenciled interior is more Hollywood baronial hall. The building was shoehorned into the former site of the power plant, resulting in a hall that was too short for good acoustics. The situation worsened with the donation of the sesquicentennial organ by Cyrus Curtis. Its incorporation into an added tower spelled the final doom for the acoustical goals of the hall. For three generations the building languished, until 1997, when it was brilliantly modified and adapted by Venturi, Scott Brown and Associates. Working with acoustical engineer George Izenour, they cut off the side wings from the main hall, added an acoustical brow over the stage, and hung operable banners within the tower to make it possible to "tune" the building to the type of performance. The side wings became a needed café and small recital hall. The main hall has been restored to its visual brilliance while functioning for the first time as a successful auditorium.

OPPOSITE: *William B. Irvine Auditorium*

## 10. Houston Hall

*William C. Hays (1895) and Milton B. Medary (1891), with Frank Miles Day and Brother, 1894–1896*

Recognizing the dearth of positive activities for students on the late-nineteenth-century campus, Provost Harrison organized a competition among Penn's architecture students for the design of a student union. The winning students presented two schemes: one reflected the post-Columbian exposition interest in Spain while the other was modeled on the late-English Gothic Peacock Inn at Rowley, Yorkshire, doubtless because its domestic Gothic flavor conformed to Cope and Stewardson's projected design for the new dormitory quadrangles. The latter scheme was selected by a national panel of architects, helping to determine the future course of campus design.

The program requirement for a monumental stair was met in the paired stairs that flank the entrance to the central room. Wood paneling and at least one fireplace in each major room convey the nostalgic tone of the building, which has worn well over the years. The central hall was flanked by a game room with pool tables at one end and a reading room at the other; dining and meeting rooms occupied much of the upper level with a theater in one wing, while the basement included a gymnasium and swimming pool.

As the university community expanded from 1,000, many of the athletic functions moved to new quarters. By the 1930s the Commons Room and the John Houston Lounge were seamlessly added by Robert Rhodes McGoodwin. Houston Hall is named for Henry Howard Houston, Jr. (1878), son of the vice president of the Pennsylvania Railroad in whose memory the building was dedicated. A portrait of the young Houston by Cecelia Beaux ornaments the west lounge.

Beginning in 1995 Houston Hall was restored by Venturi, Scott Brown and Associates as the centerpiece of the Perelman Quadrangle. The firm re-created the removed stair of the central hall, removed partitions that divided the original lounge and game room, and returned the interior to its historic color schemes. The architects emphasized the new role of the hall as the center for the Perelman Quad with the information desk that dominates the space. It provides up-to-date information about campus activities. Departing from the deference accorded to the public spaces, the architects treated the basement as found space, transforming it to a modern food court that provides numerous dining options in an edgy modern setting.

OPPOSITE: *Houston Hall*

## 11. Edwin B. and Leonore R. Williams Humanities and Language Hall *Nolen, Swinburne, and Associates, 1972*

*Edwin B. and Leonore R. Williams Humanities and Language Hall*

Williams Hall occupies the site of Thomas Richards's Hare Laboratories, which were demolished in 1972. Like many of the buildings of its era, it turned its back on the street to face inward toward the main campus. This was doubly unfortunate because the north-facing courtyard that resulted was cold and unpleasant, a difficulty remedied by the bright hues of the Silfern Study Center by Venturi, Scott Brown and Associates. Between Houston Hall and Williams Hall is the Class of 1893 Memorial Gate designed in 1900 by two members of the class, Elliston P. Bissell and the co-winner of the Houston Hall competition, William C. Hays. The motto of the class, "We shall find a way or we shall make one" could serve as the motto of the university.

## 12. Logan Hall

*Thomas W. Richards, 1873–1874;*
*adaptive restoration, Venturi, Scott Brown and Associates, 1995–1998*

Logan Hall was built to house the Medical School with large amphitheaters for teaching on the east side and offices across the west front. The architect retained the Gothic detail of College Hall but simplified the silhouette to represent the campus hierarchy. The entrance was given its due with flanking granite columns that support the projecting central bay. More "muscular" than College Hall, it represented the single use of the Medical School in its compact form. With the completion of the John Morgan Building in 1906, medicine moved to Hamilton Walk, and the old building was renamed for Penn's colonial secretary James Logan and occupied by the Wharton School. At that time, the immense auditoria of the old Medical School were replaced with a modern concrete frame that was clad in cast-stone blocks faced with serpentine aggregate. After Wharton left for its new quarters in 1952, the building housed a variety of academic services and departments. Its rehabilitation by Venturi, Scott Brown and Associates as the home of the college underscores Penn's dedication to undergraduate education as the centerpiece of President Rodin's Agenda for Excellence.

*Logan Hall*

## 13. Locust Walk East

**E. Craig Sweeten Alumni Center**
*Elliston P. Bissell, John P. B. Sinkler, and Marmaduke Tilden, 1914*
**Jerome Fisher Program in Management** *Lester Kintzing, 1913*
**Phi Kappa Sigma** *Elliston P. Bissell and John P. B. Sinkler, 1909*
**Alpha Chi Rho** *Alfred B. Kister, 1916*

A cluster of small buildings occupies the remaining quadrant along the former 36th and Locust streets. Built as fraternities in the early twentieth century, they were linked by materials and detail to the contemporary image of the university. The E. Craig Sweeten Alumni Center, formerly 3533 Locust Walk, was designed in 1914 by Elliston P. Bissell, John P. B. Sinkler, and Marmaduke Tilden, all graduates of the university's School of Architecture. In 1981, it was adapted by later Penn graduates Charles Dagit and Peter Saylor to serve as the offices of the alumni society. The Jerome Fisher Program in Management occupies 3557 Locust Walk, a refaced Victorian house updated in the campus Gothic by Lester Kintzing (Arch. 1900) in 1913. At the corner of the former 36th Street, Phi Kappa Sigma was built in 1909. Fraternity members Elliston P. Bissell and John P. B. Sinkler designed its handsome classically detailed house. Around the

TOP: *E. Craig Sweeten Alumni Center*
BOTTOM: *Alpha Chi Rho*

*Phi Kappa Sigma*

corner on 36th Street is the subdued Gothic facade of Alpha Chi Rho by
Alfred B. Kister (Arch. 1910), which dates from 1916. These buildings form
a bridge to the fraternities that continue west on Locust Walk to the residential community beyond.

# West Central Campus

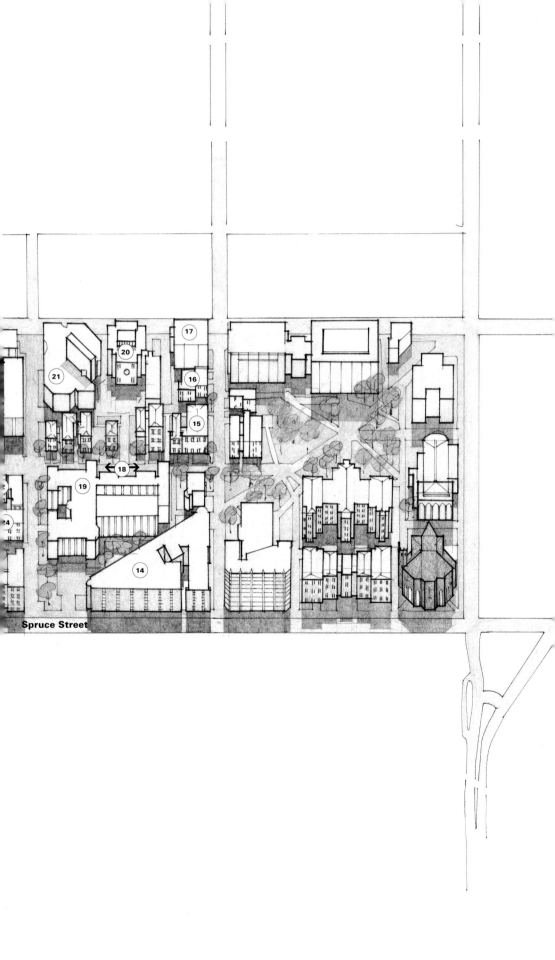

Spruce Street

The western portion of the central campus first evolved in the 1890s when the university built the Wistar Institute on the wedge of land between Woodland Avenue and Spruce Street, west of 36th Street. In the early twentieth century, Penn-related fraternities began buying properties along Locust Street, creating fraternity row. By the 1920s the majority of houses east of 38th Street were owned by student groups and university-affiliated organizations such as the Christian Association. Those changes were premonitions of what would come later with the 1948 master plan that turned the university from the northward course of the Cret plan to the present-day westward course. This shift began to take place almost immediately with the acquisition of the site for the Wharton School's Dietrich Hall in 1949 and has continued with the filling of every principal site over the last half century.

After World War II, urban renewal transformed the scale and pace of Penn's growth. All of the property between Spruce and Walnut streets and additional swaths along Market Street were acquired by condemnation, enabling Penn planners to think on a regional scale rather than project by project. Even before urban renewal made this possible, Penn architects had begun to dream of a vastly larger campus. An aerial perspective prepared for the 1948 master plan shows a slender skyscraper for the central administration at 36th Street, while Locust Street was to be transformed into a pedestrian walk with the future Dietrich Hall on the south and the Christian Association and fraternities on the north. Small residential quadrangles filled in between Locust Street and Walnut Street; beyond 37th Street, open playing fields were to line both sides of the continuing walk with additional men's residential quadrangles along Walnut Street. Freudian psychologists would have had a field day with the U-shaped women's dormitory beyond 38th Street that was to form the end of Locust Walk.

A second master plan from the early 1960s revised the 1948 plan, pushing undergraduate housing west across 38th Street while reserving the space to the east for academic purposes. It was this plan that has largely been implemented. With the current construction of the Wharton School's Huntsman Hall on the site of a small Penn strip mall, there are now no more open spaces. Future changes will require demolition or removal from the central campus.

## 14. Wistar Institute of Anatomy, Woodland Walk, and Psi Upsilon

### Wistar Institute of Anatomy, Psi Upsilon
*George W. Hewitt and William D. Hewitt, 1892–1894 and 1897*
**Woodland Walk** *Ian McHarg*

Built to house the anatomical specimens collected by the premier anatomist of the early nineteenth-century United States, Caspar Wistar, M.D., the Wistar Institute is the nation's oldest independent biomedical research institute. The contrast between the Hewitt Brothers' Institute and the University Library, which had just been completed across campus from designs by their former partner, Frank Furness, anticipated the post–World War II battle between the International Stylists' doctrine of "Universal Space" and the particularized shaping of space by Louis I. Kahn and his followers. The institute contrasts at every point with Furness's highly explicit design. From the light-toned yellow brick and limestone-hued terra-cotta of the facade to the logical factory-like steel-frame structure, Wistar reflects the underlying order of classicism that is clearly affirmed in the subtly projecting entrance on 36th Street. Within, massive steel girders span from side to side, making it possible to adapt the interior as later functions have required. Additions by the Hewitts in 1897 and the massive laboratory wing by Mansell, Lewis and Fugate of 1975 have completely filled in the triangle formed by Woodland Avenue.

With the closing of Woodland Avenue along the rear of the Wistar Institute, Woodland Walk was created as a series of small squares densely

*Wistar Institute of Anatomy*

*Psi Upsilon*

planted with flowering trees. This was the first project on campus of Penn Professor Ian McHarg, whose seminal publication *Design With Nature* marked the rise of ecological planning.

North of Woodland Walk, 36th Street continues the residential scale of the Victorian neighborhood. The first purpose-built fraternity on campus, Psi Upsilon ("The Castle"), was designed in 1897 by George W. Hewitt and William D. Hewitt, whose son John was a member. Constructed at the same time as Houston Hall, just before the shift to brick at the Quad, the blocky and vertical massing of Psi Upsilon continued Victorian design habits while incorporating the historically accurate detailing of the next generation.

### 15. ARCH Building

*Walter Thomas (Arch. 1899), Sydney Martin (Arch. 1907), Donald M. Kirkpatrick (Arch. 1911), 1927–1929*

The ARCH Building (Arts, Research, and Culture House), formerly known as the Christian Association, is the most lyrical of the late-Gothic revival buildings of the campus. It reflects the subtle detail and adroit compositions of Edwin Lutyen's turn-of-the-century English country houses that interested Philadelphia suburban architects in the 1920s. A remarkable array of dormers and chimneys enlivens the roof while large volumes contrast with small entrance pavilions. The heightened picturesque of the

*ARCH Building*

design is amplified by the delicate in situ–carved French limestone portals and oriels. Built to house the Christian Association, which served the then religiously divided, socially stratified, and largely male under-graduate community, the richly detailed interior contained club-rooms, a theater, and a small chapel. Now owned by the university, it has been adapted to include administrative offices and student facilities as well as restaurants that are open to the public.

### 16. Hillel Foundation *Arthur E. Davis, Jr., 1925*

The last of the Gothic fraternities of the campus, this Tudor revival house was built for Delta Sigma Phi. Acquired by the Hillel Foundation as a center for Jewish students, it was doubled with a post-modern wing in contextual brick and limestone in 1983–1985 by GBQC Architects. Soon to be replaced by a new Hillel building on 39th Street behind the Fels Center, a new use will be found for the present building to complement its role as an impor-tant campus entrance.

*Hillel Foundation*

*Addams Hall*

## 17. Addams Hall

*Hatfield, Martin and White, 1957–1959; Maria Romañach, 2000–2001*

Addams Hall was constructed as the faculty club in 1957–1959 from designs
of three of Paul Cret's students. As could be expected from their beaux-arts
training, their scheme was more about the fashionable elements of the style
than truly rooted in the convictions of modern design. The facade is self-
consciously asymmetrical to meet conventions of modern design, but the
marble-lined brick piers separating registers of pink marble spandrels and
windows were derived from such early modernists as Eliel Saarinen. A
quiet garden entrance was the best feature. Maria Romañach replaced
much of the fictive stone facade with a skin of clipped-on opaque and clear
glass panels that light interior studios for the undergraduate fine arts and
design programs. In the entrance are cutouts of Charles Addams's cartoon
figures that memorialize the gift of the widow of the *New Yorker* magazine's
famed cartoonist, who attended Penn's School of Fine Arts in the 1930s.

**18. Locust Walk** *George Patton, landscape architect, 1957*

**3609–11 Locust Walk** *Samuel Sloan, c. 1873*

**Locust House, 3643 Locust Walk**

  *c. 1872, renovated by Voith & Mactavish Architects, 1996*

**Graduate Center, 3615 Locust Walk** *Abraham Levy (Arch. 1920), 1951*

**Phi Gamma Delta, 3619–21 Locust Walk** *Walter Mellor and Arthur Meigs, 1913*

**Delta Phi, 3627 Locust Walk** *Wright, Andrade and Amenta, 1959*

**Delta Psi, 3637 Locust Walk** *Cope and Stewardson, 1907*

**Colonial Penn Center, 3641 Locust Walk**

  *Frank Rommel and Francis Gugert, 1904–1905,*

  *rehabilitation Eshbach, Glass, Kale and Associates, 1973*

The first step toward creating the modern Penn campus was initiated in 1957 when Locust Street was closed and repaved in a decorative interlace of brick and cobblestones. Now lined with mature trees, it is the main route between the western residential campus and the central facilities of the university. Along Locust Walk are buildings that tell of Penn's westward expansion. 3609–11 Locust Walk are part of a row of brownstone-fronted, mansarded townhouses (c. 1873) attributed to pattern-book author Samuel Sloan. At the west end of the block is a porch-fronted Second Empire twin now called Locust House at 3643 (c. 1872, renovated by Voith & Mactavish Architects, 1996), which serves women's groups. It survives from the middle-class suburb that developed near the horse-car lines that provided access to the downtown. In between are buildings that were constructed as fraternities, adapting the university brick and limestone to contemporary fashion. The

*Locust House*

TOP: *Colonial Penn Center and Delta Psi*
BOTTOM: *Delta Psi and Delta Phi*

LEFT: *Graduate Center*
RIGHT: *Phi Gamma Delta*

Graduate Center (3615), a recent adaptation to serve graduate students, was designed in 1951 by Abraham Levy to replace the Phi Sigma Kappa house that was demolished for the construction of the Wharton School across Locust Street. Its strident asymmetry, cantilevered canopy, and corner windows on the upper stories are hallmarks of 1920s modernism in the hands of a Paul Cret–trained classicist. Built in 1913 for Phi Gamma Delta by Walter Mellor and Arthur Meigs, 3619–21 Locust Walk is the counterpart to the Christian Association (now the ARCH Building) in sophistication, speaking the same language of old money and good historically based design. Gothic in detail with its chapter room fronting Locust Street and a sheltered entrance back from the then busy street, it is a tiny masterpiece by the city's leading architects of suburban nostalgia. West of Phi Gamma Delta is Delta Phi by Wright, Andrade and Amenta. It was built in 1959 to house the St. Elmo Club, the oldest of the university fraternities, which was established on the 9th Street campus in 1849. Its Georgian revival proportions attest to the architects' training before the triumph of modernism after World War II, but the projecting Flemish bond brickwork looks forward to post-modern irony. Appropriately, its neighbor at 3637 Locust Walk is Penn's second oldest fraternity, Delta Psi. Their house with side yard was designed in 1907 by the campus architects Cope and Stewardson. It is a restrained but remarkably elegant version of the campus style that addresses the moment before the Gothic was overwhelmed by Renaissance classicism. The Colonial Penn Center at 3641 Locust Walk was built for Phi Kappa Psi in 1904–1905 by alumni Frank Rommel and Francis Gugert, who associated for the project. The clumsy rehabilitation by Eshbach, Glass, Kale and Associates removed a splendid arts and crafts interior.

*Steinberg–Dietrich Hall*

### 19. Steinberg-Dietrich Hall

*McKim, Mead, and White, 1949; Warner, Burns, Toan and Lunde, 1980–1982*

In 1949, Penn began its westward march with the construction of a new
building for the Wharton School, the Department of Finance and Economy.
McKim, Mead, and White's lead designer, James Kellum Smith, had graduated from Penn's architecture program in 1918; in Smith's hands Dietrich
Hall was moderne with touches of Saarinen and even late Wright in a generally symmetrical composition. As its style fell from favor,
it was refaced, refenestrated, and renamed Steinberg-Dietrich Hall for
Wharton graduate Saul Steinberg. Dissatisfied with the results, the university commissioned Penn faculty and landscape architects Robert Hanna and
Laurie Olin to screen the blank facade with a handsome pergola that owes
its timber detailing to Greene and Greene's California work.

### 20. Annenberg School for Communication

*Albert Easton Poor, 1962; Mitchell/Giurgola Architects, 1982; MGA Architects 1998–2000*

On axis with Steinberg-Dietrich Hall, with its principal entrance off Locust Walk
is the Annenberg School for Communication. The school owes its existence to a
gift from publisher Walter Annenberg, who also selected the original architect,
Alfred Easton Poor (Arch. 1924). Poor's 1962 scheme faced a simply detailed
limestone-clad building toward a south plaza created by closing the north-south
street, away from the noise of Walnut Street. In 1982, Mitchell/Giurgola

TOP: *Annenberg School for Communication, redesign of north facade, MGA Partners*
BOTTOM: *Walnut Street entrance, MGA Partners*

Architects extended the building to the south behind a taut symmetrical screen whose red stone accents ironically reverse the proportions of color of earlier Penn buildings. The plaza was excavated for classrooms and replaced by a sculpted stone deck whose intersecting lines of multicolored stone and raised central ring complement the facade composition. Most recently, the successor firm MGA Partners has redesigned the north facade. Its creation of a new front and an entrance courtyard on Walnut Street is part of Penn's rethinking of its relation to the main streets that run through the campus.

Within are Sam Maitin's (1951) brightly hued construction *Celebration* (1976, enlarged in 1985) and Jose de Rivera's *Construction 66* (1959, installed 1963). A splendid bronze tensile structure by Henry Bertoia, entitled *Homage to Performing Art* (1975), is suspended in the main lobby.

### 21. Annenberg Center *Vincent Kling and Associates, 1971*

Walter Annenberg's munificence continued with this understated perform-ing arts center designed by Vincent Kling and Associates—the architect whose work transformed center city Philadelphia after World War II. At once complementary and contrasting to the first school building, its brown brick walls enclose the fly lofts and auditorium shapes of three theaters of vary-ing sizes that share a central lobby. The center houses performances of modern dance, which require full staging capacity, and plays an important role in the experimental theater and dance traditions of the city.

*Annenberg Center*

*Phi Delta Theta*

## 22. Phi Delta Theta and Kappa Sigma

**Phi Delta Theta, 3700 Locust Walk**
*Robert Rhodes McGoodwin (1907, Arch. 1908), 1924*
**Kappa Sigma, 3706 Locust Walk** *Theodore Epps (Arch. 1919), 1924*

Across 37th Street, Locust Walk continues with two additional fraternities that maintain the residential cadence of the old street and share the Penn palette. Unlike the Gothic style of the early twentieth-century fraternities of the 3600 block, the choice of the colonial revival style reflects the regional impact of the sesquicentennial celebration of the nation's independence of 1926. Phi Delta Theta at 3700 Locust Walk is a 1924 design by Robert Rhodes McGoodwin, a brother in the fraternity during its years at 34th Street and Woodland Avenue. Its corner site caused the architect to devise two facades, one facing Locust Street through a two-story Corinthian portico screened by a low wall and the other featuring large gabled wings flanking a central entrance addressing 37th Street. Kappa Sigma at 3706 Locust was designed by brother Theodore Epps in 1924. Its blocky early Georgian facade and massive scrolled door surround epitomize the masculine world of the male fraternity in its heyday on Locust Street.

## 23. Lehman Brothers Quadrangle and Vance Hall

**Lehman Brothers Quadrangle** *Hanna-Olin Ltd., 1991*
**Vance Hall** *Bower (Arch. 1953) and Fradley, 1971–1973*

Thirty-seventh Street has been incorporated into the campus and now forms a transition between portions of the Wharton School. To the east is a courtyard that is the best surviving bit of the McKim, Mead and White design for Dietrich Hall. Across 37th Street is the Lehman Brothers Quadrangle, a 1991 landscape by Hanna-Olin Ltd. Just off Locust Walk is George W. Lunden's seated bronze figure of *Ben Franklin on Campus* (1987) reading the *Gazette* instead of the *Daily Pennsylvanian*. With extra room on the bench, it is a popular site for snapshots.

The preliminary scheme for Vance Hall called for it to house the campus mainframe computer, then housed in an industrial building on Market Street. Its design incorporates the contemporary brutalist vocabulary of

TOP: *Vance Hall*
BOTTOM LEFT: *Lehman Brothers Quadrangle*
BOTTOM RIGHT: *37th Street and Locust Walk*

poured-in-place concrete columns and slabs infilled with panels of red brick similar to Kahn's work at the Richards building. North-facing glass walls would dissipate the heat generated by the computer, while projecting concrete sun screens across the Spruce Street facade would further reduce the heat load. While it was being planned, miniaturization reduced the size and energy requirements of computers, making it unnecessary to have a purpose-built home. The architects were asked to adapt the design to serve as a graduate classroom building for the Wharton School, continuing that program's western advance toward 38th Street. To accommodate the larger population of a classroom building, glass-skinned stairs recalling the by then iconic Bauhaus were incorporated at the corridor ends. A lounge at the west end, featuring a poured-in-place coffered concrete ceiling and a fireplace with window above, quotes Louis Kahn's canonical works, notably the ceiling of the Yale Art Gallery and the fireplace of the Esherick House in Chestnut Hill.

### 24. Lauder-Fischer Building *Davis and Brody, 1988–1990*

Although it is the work of one of Penn's best-known modernist graduates, Lewis Davis, the contextual character of the Lauder-Fischer Hall reveals its later date. The slate-gabled roof and Flemish bond brickwork relate to the 37th Street facade of Phi Delta Theta, but the corner and strip windows assert the modern values of the architects by expressing the underlying skeleton. Containing the Joseph Lauder Institute of Management and International Studies, and the Fischer Real Estate Program, it is an integral part of the Wharton campus.

*Lauder–Fischer Building*

*Aresty–Steinberg Hall*

### 25. Aresty-Steinberg Hall *Hillier Group, 1988*

The Wharton entrepreneurial spirit is well-represented by the school's decision to build a conference center for its many executive programs. The center contains a floor of meeting rooms with a hotel above. Contrasting with the architectural gravitas of Vance Hall, the facade is more Bartletts' *Familiar Quotations* than high architecture. The twin towers, massive gates, and polychromed masonry of the west front recall the Quad even though in a post-modern vein, while the muted hues of the masonry and the teal blue-green windows are derived from the commercial architecture of the highway.

### 26. Huntsman Hall *Kohn Pedersen Fox, 1997–2002*

The dominance of the early twentieth-century campus by engineering and medicine was reflected by the construction of Penn's largest classroom buildings; at the beginning of the twenty-first century, business and finance are exceeded only by the college as the university's largest program—a fact attested to by the size of Huntsman Hall, which looms above Walnut Street at the west end of the campus. In their office towers and commercial projects, Kohn Pedersen Fox have become masters of strongly sculptural statements that give instant identity in the commercial landscape. At Huntsman Hall, they strive heroically to achieve visual distinction by bringing together

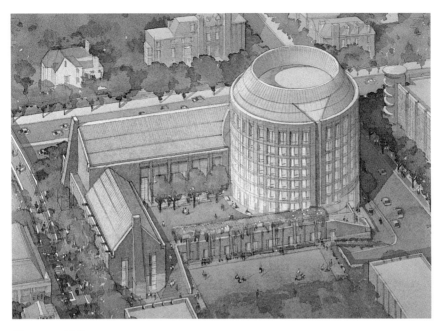

*Huntsman Hall*

an array of strongly differentiated volumes at a vast scale. Where the Philadelphia School masters of the 1960s and 1970s derived form from the specific requirements of function, the post-modern adaptation assembles forms to represent the outlines of the program. All undergraduate classes are in the lower levels, graduate courses are taught in the mid-zone, and the faculty offices are in the tower. In art historical jargon, the building is the reification of the Wharton hegemony. The buttress-like fins of the 38th Street front are vaguely Gothic, the massive chimney-like stack at the end of the main gable gives this part of the building the appearance of a super-sized Virginia plantation house, while the red hues of brick and cleaved stone recall Furness's library.

### 27. Social Sciences Quadrangle

*Harbeson, Hough, Livingston and Larson, 1965–1966*

The Social Sciences Quadrangle offers a glimpse of the campus as it would have appeared if the 1948 master plan had been followed. Small spaces are framed by buildings of related purpose and modest size. Ordering, pilaster-like piers recall the beaux-arts training of their architects. Following the model of the central campus, the backs were turned to the street while the fronts faced into an interior courtyard. A teahouse-like lounge in the court was intended as a place where informal discussion would bridge the

TOP: *Social Sciences Quadrangle*
BOTTOM: *McNeil Building*

separate departments. Ruled by a grid that extends into the paving pattern of the concrete plaza, there is more of Brasilia than the Renaissance here. A new Walnut Street front and revised fenestration were designed by Ewing Cole Cherry Brott in 2001.

### 28. McNeil Building *Ballinger Company, 1964–1970*

Viewed from Locust Walk and from within its dour first-floor lobby, the McNeil Building, like the Social Sciences Quadrangle and other buildings funded by the Pennsylvania's General State Authority, is more utility than poetry. However, above the lobby the upper stories of offices and class-rooms look into an astonishing interior space. Known to few in the university, it is a tour de force of the spatial potential of modern construction. Four stories of offices are grouped around a central atrium that is surrounded by balconies that are served by a concrete stair cantilevered from a central column. The Ballinger Company has been known for a century for their design of clear span industrial spaces such as this.

# East Campus

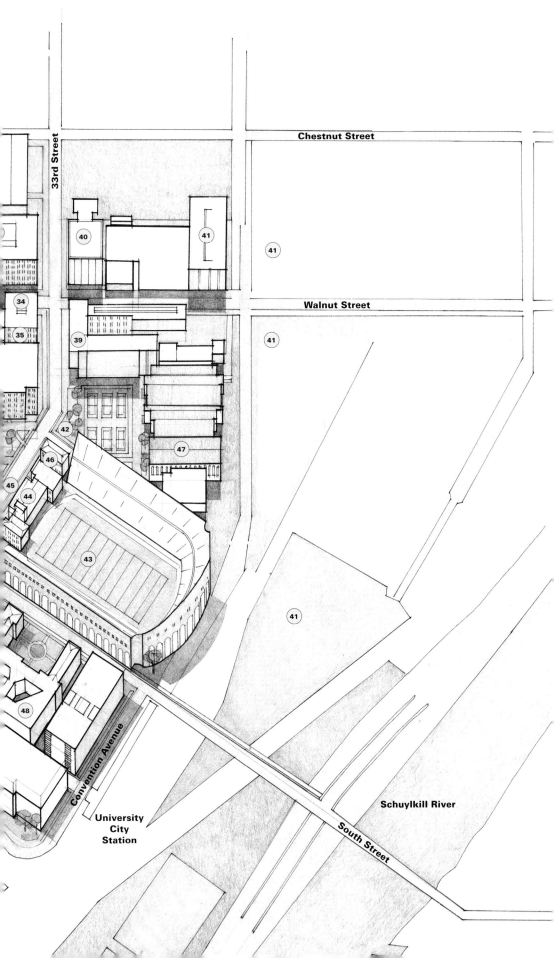

Chestnut Street

Walnut Street

33rd Street

Convention Avenue

University
City
Station

South Street

Schuylkill River

The property to the east of 34th Street remained a part of the city's Blockley Almshouse grounds into the 1880s, when Provost Pepper proposed to the city that land facing the university along 34th Street be made available for educational and other related institutions. The first organization to take advantage of the free land was the Foulke and Long Institute, which commissioned a school and residence for the orphaned children of Civil War veterans in 1890. Penn later acquired these buildings for its physics program. A year later, in 1891, the university-affiliated Lea Institute of Hygiene was built where the Vagelos Labs now stand. Although these buildings were sited to leave space for Locust Street, which was already on the city plan, the street was never opened. In 1893, the university built its first independent chemistry classroom and laboratory building at the corner of Spruce Street, filling the final open space facing 34th Street.

The next buildings were sited along the projected route of Locust Street, beginning with the first purpose-built school of dentistry in the country (now Hayden Hall). Across from the Dental School, the Towne Building was constructed to house engineering, the university's largest undergraduate program at that time. Towne was the largest building of the campus and was designed in the dark red brick with limestone detail of the Harrison era. It filled the last important open space and made it unlikely that Locust Street would ever be opened. The landscape by Cope and Stewardson was part of the Towne project; its tree-lined bluestone walks hinted at the campus of the future.

The Cold War led to an expansion of the sciences, reflected by the construction of new buildings for the chemistry, electrical engineering, and graduate programs. Where the Victorian moderns developed separate academic disciplines, post-moderns have focused on the connections between fields. This evolution is represented in the east science precinct by the Laboratory for Research on the Structure of Matter (LRSM) at 33rd and Walnut streets and the Vagelos Laboratories, each linking their neighboring disciplines in the applied and basic sciences.

The sculptures in the precinct depict scientists. In the plaza at 34th Street, faculty member R. Tait McKenzie's (1926) seated figure of Professor of Chemistry and Provost Edgar Fahs Smith can be found. In the handsome mid-block park by Olin Partners is a standing figure of chemist John Harrison (1773–1833) by Lynn Jenkins (1934). It portrays the founder of the Harrison Chemical Works, whose fortune supported the sciences at Penn.

LEFT: *Morgan Building*
RIGHT: *Music Building*

## 29. Morgan and Music Buildings  *Cope and Stewardson, 1890–1892*

These minor masterpieces by Cope and Stewardson for the Foulke and
Long Institute were the first buildings to be constructed on the east side of
34th Street. Of red brick with delicately molded brick and terra-cotta detail,
they acknowledge the color scheme of Furness's University Library but contrast in their careful incorporation of historical references. The broad, overhanging hipped roofs carried on deep wooden outriggers and the pressed
terra-cotta ornamental bands are based on the early Renaissance of
Northern Italy. In the early 1890s, the architects worked in the same mode
for the nearby Harrison Chemistry Laboratory (demolished 1972) and for
various buildings at the hospital. The architects had learned the lesson of
Richardsonian simplification; this pair shows that other styles were in the
running for the campus style than just the late English Gothic of the Quad.
The university purchased the buildings in 1900 and adapted them to house
the physics program, naming them the Morgan Laboratory for their donor,
Randall Morgan (1873, M.A. 1876). Since the move of physics to the
Rittenhouse Laboratory in 1954 (see 39), the buildings have housed nursing,
music, and fine-arts related classrooms. Plans now call for them to be incorporated into the Institute for Advanced Sciences.

## 30. Roy and Diana Vagelos Laboratories of the Institute for Advanced Science and Technology
*Venturi, Scott Brown and Associates with Payette Associates, 1991–1997*

The most recent building along 34th Street is a brilliant essay in contextualism based on the hues of the red brick and brownstone of Furness's
University Library and the red brick and terra-cotta of Seeler's Dental Hall.
These materials reappear in the Vagelos Laboratories, with brownstone
accenting the base and red tiles screening the attic with red brick in
between. The varied uses of the interior are evident from the fenestration.
Repetitive, oversized windows describe banks of laboratories on the sides.

TOP: *Roy and Diana Vagelos Laboratories of the Institute for Advanced Science and Technology*
BOTTOM: *Hayden Hall*

Conference rooms and other more public spaces overlook Smith Walk on the north end. In the north lobby, terra-cotta plaques from the Lea Institute of Hygiene memorialize the previous building on the site, which was funded by historian and civic leader Charles Henry Lea, who commissioned his family architects Collins and Autenreith in 1891. Their design was developed in consultation with the institute's first director, Dr. John Shaw Billings, whose study of military hospitals led to broad advances in public health. The new building is named for the Chairman of the University Board of Trustees and scientist Roy Vagelos (College 1950) and his wife, Diana, who were the lead donors of the building.

### 31. Hayden Hall *Edgar V. Seeler, 1894–1896*

Dental programs were generally little more than afterthoughts in medical schools when Seeler designed Penn's dental school more than a century ago. At Penn, however, dentistry granted the second largest numbers of degrees after medicine. The subtly varied reddish hues of the brick and the composition of bays flanking a centered entrance recall Henry Hobson Richardson's Sever Hall at Harvard, which Seeler would have known when he studied at M. I. T. Instead of Richardson's muscular Romanesque, Seeler turned toward the fashionable Queen Anne with shaped late-Gothic gables above the projecting bays in a field of Flemish bond brickwork. The structure is adapted from industrial slow-burning construction characterized by massive timbers carrying heavy planks for the flooring. Like Furness's library, stairs and other elements were pushed outside the main building envelope, freeing the floors to be divided as needed. The bays on the front contained classrooms on the first floor and small amphitheaters off the hall of practice that occupied the entire second floor. This single room measured 50 by 180 feet and was filled with dental chairs (and patients) that were aimed toward the even light of the north-facing windows.

In 1915, when the dental school moved to new quarters at 40th and Spruce streets, the great hall of practice became the atelier of the architecture program. Here, Paul Cret guided four successive Rome Prize winners before World War I and later taught architects Louis Kahn and Joseph Esherick, who shaped American architecture after World War II. Under G. Holmes Perkins, a new dean drawn from the ranks of the modernists, the grand foyer and central stair were replaced with a large room that could be used for school juries. Here Perkins's faculty—led by architects Louis Kahn, Romaldo Giurgola, and Robert Venturi; urbanist Lewis Mumford; and ecologist Ian McHarg—discussed student projects and debated the future of their crafts.

When Meyerson Hall was constructed as the new home for fine arts in 1965–1968, geology, the last of the sciences still housed in College Hall, took over the old Dental School. The building was renamed once again, this time for geologist and Penn faculty member Ferdinand Hayden. After the Civil War, Hayden headed the United States Geological and Geographical Survey, and his explorations led to the designation of the Yellowstone region as the first national park.

## 32. Chemistry Laboratories

**Chemistry Building**
*Ballinger Company with Harbeson, Hough, Livingston, and Larson, 1969–1973*
**Cret Chemistry Building** *Paul P. Cret, 1940*
**John Harrison Chemistry Laboratory** *Harbeson, Hough, Livingston, and Larson, 1958*

The present elephantine, vibration-proof structure is the work of a firm noted for innovations in industrial design such as the industrial applications of reinforced concrete and the super-span truss. Its concrete frame is sheathed with the contextual Flemish-bond brickwork that characterized much of Penn's architecture of the 1970s. In the first-floor lobby, memorials of the history of the chemistry program are displayed. The most notable is a portrait of *John Harrison*, grandfather of Provost Harrison, by Mary Jean Peale, a member of the ubiquitous Peale family of artists. The splendid Italianate frame is a memento of the Italian details of Cope and Stewardson's Chemistry Building, which stood on the site of the present laboratories. Hanging in the well that links the upper and lower lobbies is Robert Engman's cast aluminum sculpture *After Iyengar* (1977).

At the rear of the Chemistry Building are two wings that once were attached to Cope and Stewardson's first chemistry building. At the corner of 33rd and Spruce streets is the Cret Chemistry Building of 1940–1941. It is the only design on campus by Paul Cret, who was the professor of design in the School of Fine Arts from 1903 until 1929. Unlike Cret's better-known classically inspired works, the horizontal strips of windows and the curved corner of the laboratory were influenced by Howe and Lescaze's landmark PSFS skyscraper. The limestone and brick idiom links the building to the remainder of the campus. To its rear along 33rd Street is the John Harrison Chemistry Laboratory of 1958–1959, which was designed by Elizabeth Rottenberg (Arch. 1936)—Penn's first woman architecture graduate, who worked in the office of Cret's successor firm, Harbeson, Hough, Livingston, and Larson. Named for chemist John Harrison (M.D. 1830), the building now shows the results of alterations by Ellenzweig, Moore and Associates in the 1980s. The present patterned stucco infill of the windows and the sky-line of stainless steel exhausts identify the enterprise of science as a progressive undertaking that pays attention to the health of its workers.

TOP: *Chemistry Building*
BOTTOM: *Cret Chemistry Building*

*Towne Building*

### 33. Towne Building *Cope and Stewardson, 1903–1906*

The School of Engineering and Applied Science is centered in the Towne Building, which bears the name of Philadelphia industrialist, trustee, and donor, John Henry Towne. His gift enabled the university to enlarge its scientific curriculum after the Civil War. Built of the brick and limestone of the Harrison era, the building's style is derived from the seventeenth-century transition between Jacobean Gothic and Wren's classicism of England. Its planning and structure are rooted in the region's industrial architecture. Interior courts, which have since been replaced by prosaic computer labs, housed skylighted machine shops of the sort common in Philadelphia factories. Here students could learn by experience about the processes they would be supervising after graduation. Frederick Winslow Taylor, the father of Scientific Management, gave the dedicatory address for the new building and proclaimed the goals of the school: "The largest possibility, and one which does not exist for, and cannot be created by any other American university, lies in the opportunity for bringing your students in close touch and personal contact with the men who are working in and managing the great industrial establishments of Philadelphia."

    The second-floor corridor contains portraits of the men who shaped the school. John Henry Towne is represented by a portrait by William M. Hunt. Faculty represented include Professor of Civil Engineering Fairman Rogers, who championed the modern art of Thomas Eakins and the architecture of Frank Furness, and Edgar Marburg, who founded the American Society for Testing Materials at the school. Also depicted are the presidents of the Pennsylvania Railroad, J. Edgar Thompson and Thomas Scott, whose corporation supported the program with annual donations; and university trustees and machine makers and engineers William Sellers, and J. Vaughan Merrick—the chief donor for the building.

### 34. Alfred F. Moore School of Electrical Engineering

*George S. Morris and Richard Erskine, 1909*

*Alfred F. Moore School of Electrical Engineering*

As the birthplace of ENIAC, the world's first large-scale electronic computer, in February 1946, Penn's Moore School is a site of global significance. In addition, the building tells other tales in the evolution of the campus. The city sold property along Walnut Street to private owners for a variety of purposes, including large townhouses at 34th Street. In 1909, the massive, reinforced concrete Pepper Musical Instrument factory was constructed at the corner of 33rd Street. With the support of the region's industrial base, it was acquired by the Department of Electrical Engineering, which became a separate school in 1923. In 1926, a gift from Alfred Fitler Moore enabled the department to move from the Towne Building to the factory. Moore began manufacturing telegraph wire in the 1870s and, by the 1920s, was one of the city's principal suppliers of electrical equipment. Fortunately, the factory architects had clad their building in Flemish bond brickwork, making it possible for Paul Cret's office to adapt the building to its campus use with minimal changes. The most notable among these is the addition of the classical door frames at the entrances. The rugged, reinforced concrete construction of the original factory permitted the addition of a third floor in the 1940s by Alfred Bendiner (formerly of Cret's office). The Moore School has now rejoined the Towne School to form the School of Engineering and Applied Science. Inside its main entrance is a small museum displaying portions of the original ENIAC. It was the size of a tractor trailer but increased the speed of calculations 1,200 times, setting off the computer age.

## 35. Harold E. Pender Labs

*Geddes, Brecher, Qualls and Cunningham, 1958–1960*

*Harold E. Pender Labs*

On 33rd Street between the Towne Building and the Moore School are the Harold E. Pender Laboratories. Named for the Moore School's first dean, Harold Pender, this building links the former instrument factory with the Towne School. Like Kahn's contemporary Richards Building, Geddes, Brecher, Qualls and Cunningham used a prefabricated, reinforced concrete frame to both articulate the facade and provide clear span interior spaces. Panels of Flemish bond brickwork at each end echo the colors and textures of the adjoining Moore and Towne Buildings. This early contextual design announced the principles of the "Philadelphia School" of architectural design.

## 36. Graduate Research Center

*Geddes, Brecher, Qualls and Cunningham, 1966*

*Levine Hall and Graduate Research Center, Kieran Timberlake Associates*

Facing Walnut Street is the Moore School's Graduate Research Center, a 1966 work by Geddes, Brecher, Qualls and Cunningham. The center's interior is screened behind a curtain wall of dark, reflective glass. Vertical circulation and services are contained in contrasting corner piers, and again express characteristics of the Philadelphia School. The Graduate Research Wing is linked to the Towne Building by the glittering glass and metal facade of Levine Hall by Kieran Timberlake Associates, which was still under construction at the time of publication.

*Bennett Hall*

## 37. Bennett Hall *Stewardson and Page, 1924–1925*

Bennett Hall is the odd building in the science group. Originally constructed to house the women's programs of the university, it occupies the site of houses given to the university to encourage the education of women by Joseph Bennett, a manufacturer of Civil War uniforms. By 1924, Bennett's endowment was sufficient to pay for a new building, resulting in Stewardson and Page's understated fusion of Tudor and moderne. Its beveled facade was part of Paul Cret's plan to form a plaza at 34th and Walnut streets that was to become the main entrance to the campus. Although women had been accepted in some courses at the university as early as 1876, they remained marginalized in the institution.

Bennett Hall housed all of the women's facilities, including the School of Education (then largely composed of women). The Maria Hosmer Penniman Library, devoted to education, filled the great two-story hall above the main entrance. With the removal of its collection to Van Pelt Library, it has been converted into a lecture room. Bennett Hall also contained the women's student union in the basement and the women's gymnasium on the fourth floor. The number of Ivy Day plaques on the building marks Bennett Hall as the sole site where women's activities were sanctioned until the construction of a new women's dormitory, Hill Hall, across Walnut Street (see North Campus). These distinctions ended in 1966, when the College for Women merged into the College. At that time, Bennett Hall became the home of the English Department. A walk of fame (designed by Jody Pinto) celebrating the achievements of Penn's women is to be dedicated in the fall of 2001 across from the former women's precinct at 34th street above Walnut Street.

*Hill College House*

*Zeta Psi*

## 38. Hill College House (originally Hill Hall) and Zeta Psi

**Hill College House**  *Eero Saarinen and Associates, 1960*
**Zeta Psi**
> *Walter H. Thomas (Arch. 1899), Clarke W. Churchman (Arch. 1895), and John Molitor, 1909*

As Eero Saarinen's Hill College House demonstrates, Kahn was not the only architect of the 1950s to make the shift toward context and historical allusion. Saarinen's rugged perimeter fence, broad moat of green ivy, and entrance from a drawbridge-like span give this late design something of the romance of a castle; this image is enhanced by the strongly textured cull brick, the alternating checkerboard of horizontal and vertical slit windows, and the crowning iron cornice. Within, the tables are turned in a brilliantly skylighted courtyard containing a dining room at the lower level and surrounded on the upper stories by shuttered openings that recall Mediterranean courtyards. The dining room is ornamented with N. C. Wyeth's *Apotheosis of Franklin* (1926), a highly colored exercise in myth-making by one of the masters of the Brandywine School. Hill College House is named for Robert Hill (1889), whose gift was used to buy the land.

Just west of Hill College House, on a tiny triangle of land between Walnut Street and the now removed Woodland Avenue is the fraternity house for Zeta Psi. It was built in 1909 from plans by Walter H. Thomas (1899), Clarke W. Churchman (Arch. 1899), and John Molitor. Churchman had been a member of the fraternity during his stay at the university. The scheme is familiar, recalling both the former Phi Delta Theta house (now Jaffe History of Art) and the far end of Cope and Stewardson's Quad. Unlike the careful historical detail of Phi Delta Theta and the Quad, the design of Zeta Psi shows a freedom that suggests the influence of the arts and crafts movement, which flourished around Philadelphia at the turn of the century. The crisp planes of the polygonal corner bay (containing a chapter room) and the wide mortar joints deeply recessed on the vertical abstracted carving around the door hint at the coming geometry of art deco.

## 39. David Rittenhouse Laboratories
## with Tandem Accelerator Laboratory

**David Rittenhouse Laboratories** *Office of James R. Edmunds, 1954*
**Tandem Accelerator Laboratory** *Martin, Stewart, and Noble, 1961–1962*

*David Rittenhouse Laboratories*

The science precinct crossed 33rd Street after World War II when physics moved out of the obsolete Morgan Laboratory. The architects of the David Rittenhouse Laboratories shifted from the traditional campus palette of red brick and warm limestone to orange brick and cool white marble. This and the stainless steel windows distinguish scientific modernism from the historicism of the campus. Massing and fenestration represented interior functions, drawing on Gropius's Bauhaus at Dessau, though with a modest nod toward Saarinen's General Motor's Technical Center. The exterior now suffers from a generation of modifications, but the broad, sun-filled main corridor, highlighted by brilliantly toned tiles, is a testament to the merits of the era. Carroll, Grisdale, and Van Alen designed the new wing, which was completed between 1964 and 1967. The firm's hyperactive elevation along Walnut Street hints at industrial forms and Philadelphia School meaning, but the out-of-sync details and out-of-context references to Kahn's Richards Laboratories suggest the dilemma of beaux-arts–trained architects facing a style without classical order and with different rules. The deep red brick walls trimmed in limestone and concrete mark a return to the customary palette of the historic campus that, with few exceptions, has continued to the present. At the rear is the Tandem Accelerator Laboratory, constructed in 1961–1962 by Martin, Stewart, and Noble and enlarged in 1965. Originally termed the "Betatron Building," its strident asymmetry is more "Buck Rogers" than truly functional.

*Left Bank Apartments, 3101 Walnut Street*

## 40. Laboratory for Research on the Structure of Matter (LRSM) *Martin, Stewart, Noble, and Class, 1962*

Funded by the federal government as a part of the build-up of scientific research in the Cold War, the Laboratory for Research on the Structure of Matter anticipated the post-modern reconnection of basic science disciplines for pure and applied research. The perimeter base and parapet show Penn's usual dark red brickwork, but the color scheme of yellow pebble-surfaced concrete piers against dark glass with bright blue metal work would seem more appropriate in Miami than the University of Pennsylvania campus. A hint of the Philadelphia industrial character remains in the juxtaposition of the piers (which in fact house the exhaust flues) against the glass-enclosed volume containing the open-planned laboratory floors.

## 41. Garage, Class of 1923 Ice Rink, Left Bank Apartments

**Garage** *Mitchell/Giurgola, 1964*
**Class of 1923 Ice Rink** *Robert C. McMillan Associates, 1970*
**Left Bank Apartments** *Urban Engineers, 1931; Bower, Lewis and Thrower, 2000*

In the 1960s few garages were celebrated as high architecture, but this early masterpiece by Mitchell/Giurgola warrants consideration for its poetic force. The design juxtaposes the brick screen walls along Walnut Street against

*Walnut Street Garage*

the side elevation of huge poured-in-place reinforced concrete trusses. The expressionistic contrast places this project in the realm of Philadelphia School realism and Kahn's and Robert Le Ricolais's contemporary explorations of triangulated structure. One might also see something of the romance of a Roman ruin here.

The campus continues east along Walnut Street with the Class of 1923 Ice Rink, designed in 1970 by Robert C. McMillan Associates to house Penn's short-lived hockey program. Built of reinforced concrete, much of the rink's bulk is below the raised level of Walnut Street—viewed from the street its serene horizontality is quite different than the expressionistic structure with cantilevered stairs of the lower level.

Across Walnut Street is the Left Bank, a university-partnered apartment complex housed within Pennsylvania Railroad's immense freight terminal. It was designed in the 1930s by Urban Engineers with detailing by Chicago architects Graham, Anderson, Probst and White, the successors to Daniel Burnham's office. Bower, Lewis, and Thrower Architects adapted it to its new use in 2000 by cutting out the center of the building to create an atrium overlooked by apartments. A modern elevator tower provides access to Penn's Facilities Department housed at ground level. Designed by MGA Partners, the new Facilities Offices are woven into the forest of giant concrete columns that support the upper levels (see p. xv).

The river edge is largely devoted to Penn's athletic facilities, with playing fields bordered by the rails of Amtrak. Bower Field is the principal baseball field of the university. It is reached by a handsome tubular steel truss bridge, designed by Peter McCleary of the Graduate School of Fine Arts faculty. He came to Penn to work with Robert Le Ricolais, the French master structuralist whose insights underlie much of the Philadelphia School. The bridge links Bower Field to the principal buildings of Penn's sports complex, which fronts on 33rd Street.

## 42. All Wars Memorial to Penn Alumni

*Grant Simon, architect, Charles Rudy, sculptor, 1951–1952*

*All Wars Memorial to Penn Alumni*

Mediating between the science campus on the west side of 33rd Street and the sports complex on the east is the All Wars Memorial to Penn Alumni. Combining architecture and memorial sculpture, it is rooted in the beaux-arts training of its designer, Grant Simon, who was one of Penn's pre–World War I Paris Prize winners. It was designed as a part of the 1948 campus plan and was intended as the eastern terminus of the east-west campus axis. The plan called for eliminating the old Furness-designed library and terminating the campus axis on the west in an administrative tower at 36th Street. When campus planning was taken over by the modernist Dean Perkins, such axial compositions were abandoned.

## 43. Franklin Field

*Day and Klauder with Gavin Haddin and Horace Campion,*
*associated engineers, 1922 and 1925*

From center city Philadelphia, Penn's principal visage is formed by two landmarks, the spire of Irvine Auditorium and the colossal horseshoe arcade of Franklin Field. If Irvine was a failure for half a century, Franklin Field was a triumph from its inception. The stadium tightly envelops track, field, and football with as many as 70,000 seats that are remarkable for their proximity to the action and for their sightlines. Penn sport fans believe with some justification that there may be no better stadium anywhere. The university's original playing fields at 36th and Spruce streets were replaced by the Dormitory Quadrangles. This in turn caused the athletic fields to be relocated to the east side of the campus, where they were readily accessible from downtown. The new stadium was dedicated on April 20, 1895, with the first running of the Intercollegiate and Interscholastic Relays, now known as the Penn Relays. In 1903, a low horseshoe stadium seating 20,000 was constructed from designs by Frank Miles Day and Brother, the architects of the adjacent new gymnasium, Weightman Hall. Charles Klauder, who continued Day's practice under the name of Day and Klauder, designed the present Franklin Field. The present lower stands, of

*Weightman Hall*

concrete faced with brick, were erected in 1922. The upper stands were built of steel and concrete only four years later. Their outer arcade, mounted atop that of the lower stands, gives the stadium its resemblance to the Coliseum. Completed for $500,000, it was quickly paid for by ticket sales as the average attendance rose to 60,000. It was here that such Penn stalwarts such as Reds Baignell and Chuck Bednarik played. Before Veterans Stadium was opened in 1970, the professional Philadelphia Eagles played here, shaking the campus with the crowd's mighty roar during their championship season of 1960.

## 44. Weightman Hall *Frank Miles Day and Brother, 1903–1904*

Though Day's firm is primarily remembered for suburban houses and academic commissions, it also designed factories and other industrial structures, a background that was useful for designing many of the university's athletic structures. Weightman Hall closes off the open end of the stadium. Its exterior is shaped as stumpy towers framing a building of mixed classical and medieval detail. Light-steel trusses of the sort that were common in Philadelphia factories span the interior gymnasium.

The building was funded by the athletic association and named for Dr. William Weightman, Jr. (M.D. 1867), whose will provided $50,000 for "enhancing physical education and athletics."

OPPOSITE: *Franklin Field*

I HAVE BEEN
THE MORE PARTICULAR
IN THIS DESCRIPTION OF MY JOURNEY
THAT YOU MAY COMPARE
SUCH UNLIKELY BEGINNINGS
WITH THE FIGURE
I HAVE SINCE MADE THERE

*Franklin to his Son*

BENJAMIN FRANKLIN
IN 1723

FROM
THE CLASS OF 1904
COLLEGE

## 45. Young Benjamin Franklin  *R. Tait McKenzie, 1914*

McKenzie's figure of Franklin striding into Philadelphia in 1723 recalls the university's founder as the active youth who delighted in running and swimming. The sculpture is an appropriate complement to the athletic campus, just as the icon of the Revolution fits the main campus.

## 46. White Training House  *Horace Trumbauer, 1905–1907*

*White Training House*

The extent to which Penn athletics dominated the nation under Provost Harrison is evident in the names of awards for football supremacy. John Heisman (Law 1892) played football for Penn while enrolled in the law school, and John Outland (M.D. 1902) is the namesake for the Maxwell Club's trophy for the best collegiate lineman. Penn not coincidentally had some of the nation's best facilities, leading some to claim that Penn had professionalized its teams. After a decade of success on the football field, a group of alumni commissioned Horace Trumbauer to design a training house. He worked in the mode suggested by the adjacent and recently completed Weightman Hall, designing an elegantly detailed, domestically scaled, late English Gothic structure. White Training House contains twenty-six bedrooms as well as dining and living rooms. Its name celebrates J. William White (1850–1915, M.D. 1871), founder of Penn's Department of Physical Education, team physician to the Penn football team, chair of Clinical Surgery at the hospital, and co-author of *The American TextBook of Surgery*.

## 47. Palestra and Sydney Emlen Hutchinson Gymnasium  *Day and Klauder, 1926–1928*

As the Roaring Twenties ended, Penn's intercollegiate athletic facilities occupied the largest area of the campus, thanks to the construction of Hutchinson Gymnasium and the Palestra—an indoor stadium whose name is uniquely Penn's. After discarding such names as the Coliseum, the Arena, and the Ephebeum, "Palestra" was suggested by Professor of Greek William Bates as the name of the place where Greek athletes prepared for competition.

OPPOSITE: *Young Benjamin Franklin*

*Palestra and Sydney Emlen Hutchinson Gymnasium*

As his firm had done at the earlier Weightman Hall, Charles Klauder enclosed clear-span, steel-trussed halls with vaguely historicizing facades in the red brick and light-toned trim of the Penn campus scheme. Here, details are derived from the Georgian, but smoothed and broadened in scale in an eerie anticipation of post-modernism. Like Franklin Field, the Palestra's seating tightly wraps the court, giving terrific views to all of its nearly 9,000 seats. The Palestra was the home of Penn's great basketball teams of the 1970s and 1980s, including its Final Four team of 1979 and the recent Ivy Champions of the 1990s. Its interior lobbies and concourse have been restored by Ueland, Junker, McCauley, Nicholson. They also designed the exhibit on Penn sports that includes a tribute to the "Big Five," the unique city conference of Philadelphia basketball powers: Penn, LaSalle, St. Joseph's, Temple, and Villanova. The lobby is ornamented with a pair of handsome bas reliefs by R. Tait McKenzie in 1924, one depicting a field goal and the other a plunge into the line. The Hutchinson Gymnasium was named for financier Sydney Hutchinson (1888), a trustee, former football and baseball player for the university, and chairman of the Council on Athletics. Now much altered within, Hutchinson retains the vocabulary of light steel trusses of industrial roofing.

To the side of Hutchinson Gymnasium are the Ringe Squash Courts. They were built in 1959 from plans by Paul Monaghan and named for Thomas B. Ringe (1923, Law 1926), who was president of the class of 1923.

## 48. University of Pennsylvania Museum of Archaeology and Anthropology (originally the Free Museum of Science and Art) and Hollenback Center

**University of Pennsylvania Museum of Archaeology and Anthropology**

*Wilson Eyre, Jr., Cope and Stewardson, and Frank Miles Day and Brother, associated architects, 1895–1899 with later additions. Sculpted figures by Alexander Stirling Calder*

**Hollenback Center**

*Walter Thomas, Sydney E. Martin, and Donald M. Kirkpatrick, adaptation Leon Clemmer (Arch. 1951) and Groll, 1968*

In 1888 vast discoveries made at the university-sponsored excavation at Nippur overwhelmed the available exhibition space in the new University Library. This led to the proposal for a new building that would house anthropological and archaeological collections. It was designed in a free style that owed much to the contemporary arts and crafts movement in its emphasis on handcraft and traditional materials. The tile-accented facade perhaps reflects the interests of Dr. Henry Mercer who was on the staff of the museum in its early years. Mercer would later establish the famed Moravian tile works at nearby Doylestown. An antiquarian flavor was achieved by creating a new Flemish bond composed of brick headers alternating with paired stretchers that were mortared into a unit with red pointing. The achieved

*University of Pennsylvania Museum of Archaeology and Anthropology*

LEFT: *University of Pennsylvania Museum of Archaeology and Anthropology, Mainwaring Wing*
RIGHT: *Hollenback Center*

effect was that of an immense Roman tile. This unusual technique continues through the entire historic portion of the building and was picked up by Day for the sports group across South Street. Some elements of the style, such as the great marble-framed entrance of the west courtyard, can be linked to the brick architecture of the North Italian Lombard Romanesque. Others, such as the bands of decorative tile, may be rooted in Henry Hobson Richardson's ornament at Boston's Trinity Church. The fusion of these details with beaux-arts axial planning suggests the rich potential of turn-of-the-century design before the triumph of Euro-modernism.

The building represented Harrison's view that, "It was easier when dealing with large men to do large things than small ones." Instead of conceiving a modest structure, Harrison's team planned the building as a giant filing system; separate courts would hold the product of a culture—Asia and Oceania, the Americas, and Africa (leaving European art to the Art Museum)—and each rotunda would represent an ancient civilization—Mesopotamia, Greece, and Rome. The two courtyards and rear rotunda that were built represent less than a quarter of the intended project, which was to include another court on Spruce Street, two more rotundas, and in one scheme, a mirror image of the three courts to the south. By organizing the project around separate courts, it was possible to build one wing at a time, matching growth to the expansion of the collections and the availability of funds.

The first of three intended rotundas was constructed in 1912–1915, using Gustavino tile to span the remarkable Harrison Auditorium and the towering rotunda hall above. Eastward expansion began in 1926 under the direction of Charles Klauder (Day's former partner) with the Coxe Memorial Wing and the Sharpe Wing that forms the main facade of the large courtyard. While continuing to use the general forms of round-headed windows and tile ornament, Klauder's use of saturated hues in the tiles above the entrance hint at contemporary art deco style, subtly carrying on the evolution of the building. The front gateposts of the courtyard are capped by figures representing the four continents from which collections are drawn:

Africa, Asia, North America, and Europe. They face away from the street and toward the south light as suggested by their maker, sculptor Alexander Stirling Calder.

After a hiatus of nearly half a century, in 1968 a new building program was undertaken by architects Mitchell/Giurgola. They completed the rear circulation of the Coxe and Sharpe wings, carefully working with the original vocabulary of forms and brickwork. For the Kress wing, which was to provide an entrance for school buses, they shifted to a modern scale. The east wing of the main court was completed in 2001 with the construction of the Mainwaring wing, which houses collections and provides research space for scholars. The work of Atkin, Olshin, Lawson-Bell and Associates, it again follows the general lines of the design but squeezes an additional story into the wing and shifts to a metal cladding on the side facing the city. The landscape of the splendid forecourt was restored and re-created by Olin Partnership. So, more than a century after it was begun, the museum has filled its available site.

The varied sources of the exterior mirror the collections within. Built from the base of materials recovered during the Nippur expedition—including the gold and lapis-lazuli "Ram in a Thicket" and the gilded Bull's head harp—it spans the globe from the orient to the Native Americans, providing a record of the creativity of humans over tens of thousands of years.

As a part of the museum expansion of the 1960s, Mitchell/Giurgola built the Museum Garage on the site where the outer wing of the third courtyard would have been constructed. The over-scaled "ear" of the stair enclosure on the top floor salutes the Ghibelline cornice of Franklin Field across Spruce Street. Further east, entered from the raised deck of the South Street bridge, is the Hollenback Center. It is adapted from the 1920s power plant that was built to replace Penn's earlier generator, which occupied the site where Irvine Auditorium now stands. Designed by alumni Walter Thomas, Sydney E. Martin, and Donald M. Kirkpatrick, its powerful massing expressed its function. Taking their cue from the brickwork of the nearby museum, the architects paired bricks, one above the other, to create an oversized, industrial-scale "common" bond that amplifies the scale of the building. In 1968 when the university switched to public suppliers of power, it commissioned Leon Clemmer and Groll to adapt the building for the physical education and R.O.T.C. programs. It was renamed in honor of William "Big-Bill" Hollenback (Dentistry, 1908), the All-American star of Penn's undefeated 1908 team.

# South Campus

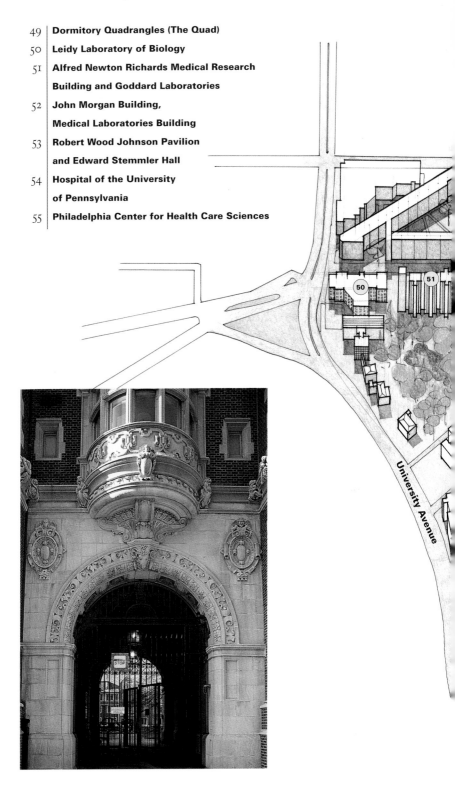

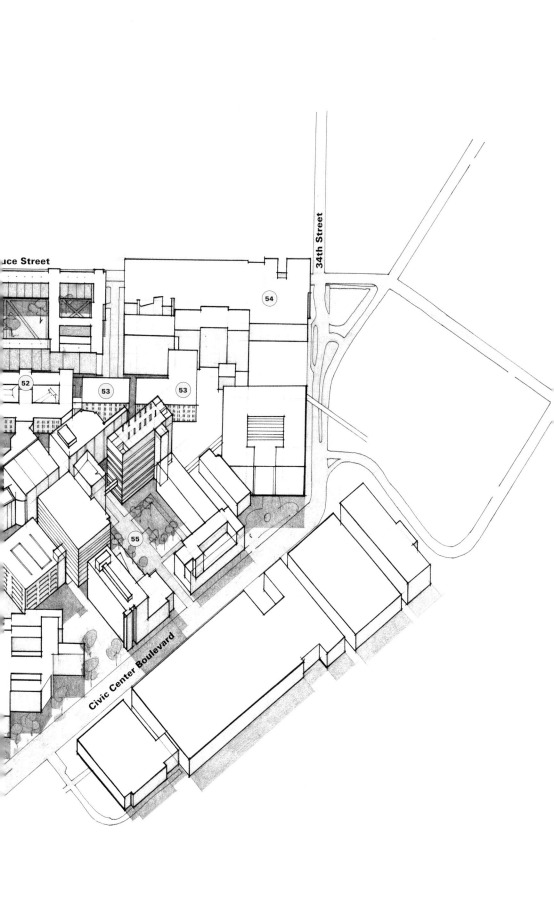

Building on the South Campus started in 1872 with the construction of the first wings of the Hospital of the University of Pennsylvania on the south side of Spruce Street. There it could share medical faculty and patients with the Blockley Almshouse, which still stood overlooking the Schuylkill River. Over the next half century, the growth of Penn's hospital was mirrored by the transformation of the almshouse into Philadelphia General Hospital (PGH). The Hospital of the University of Pennsylvania (HUP) was constructed of the green serpentine stone of the main campus. It was conceived as a pavilion-plan building with a central administrative block flanked by ward buildings. These could be augmented as needed by the addition of wards, surgeries, and other specialized functions. Over its first three decades, Penn's hospital gradually extended along Spruce Street, eventually stretching from 34th to 36th streets in a variety of styles that reflected the contemporary taste of successive generations.

To the rear of the hospital, the city plan included Pine Street, which was intersected by the diagonal of Guardian Avenue. The street's potential presence shaped the future development of the area, just as the potential of Locust Street had affected the siting of buildings in the eastern science precinct. The ghost of Pine Street remains in Hamilton Walk, which forms the spine of the block's development between 38th Street on the west and the core of the hospital at 34th Street. Penn gradually expanded its facilities in this area, trading scholarships for city residents for space to meet the growth of the medical campus. Following the general principal of proximity for related functions, the area was devoted to medical-related activities. These shortly included the Victorian Biological Hall (1884, with a third story added in 1887), which was built where the Richards Medical Research Building now stands. Established by Provost Pepper, the Biology Department launched the graduate school for advanced degrees as a part of the medical campus. Though the Biological Building was demolished in the early twentieth century, a reminder of its presence is found in the Biology Gardens.

In 1885 the Frank Furness–designed Veterinary Hospital was sited on the triangular property between Pine Street and Guardian Avenue. Its principal structure was an octagonal operating amphitheater with a raised ventilator and skylight over the operating table. Side wings along the street fronts contained stables and stalls for animals, as well as receiving offices and the gate into the enclosed court. Demolished in 1902 to make way for the John Morgan Building, the School of Veterinary Medicine then moved further west to its present location across 38th Street.

The university preserved the open space along Spruce Street west of 36th Street for its first on-campus athletic fields. Provost Harrison's vision of collegiate life on the English model required a permanent student population who would live in university dormitories. This he accomplished with the construction of the dormitory quadrangles on the sports field, stretching from 36th to 38th Street along Spruce Street and Woodland Avenue. More than any single building, the Quad, as the dormitories are affectionately known, has formed the regional and national image of the campus.

In 1902 the almshouse was separated from the hospital, which was renamed Philadelphia General Hospital. In its new role as medical center, it was replanned as a dense, mid-rise complex adjacent to Penn's medical campus. The remainder of the site became available for a new city enterprise, the Commercial Museum. Its creation was stimulated by the 1893 World's Columbian Exposition, held in Chicago, which brought together exhibits from around the world. Professor Dr. William P. Wilson, then heading the university's Biological Department, saw the possibility of acquiring the exhibits and persuaded the city to fund their purchase and eventually to house them on city property. The exhibits, it was thought, would provide models for regional industry, serving the role of the South Kensington Museum in London. Designed by the premier industrial architects of the city, the Wilson Brothers, the Commercial Museum occupied a steel-framed industrial hall, whose exterior was clad in economical white terra cotta with classical ornament that recalled the Chicago Fair.

Though the later buildings of the Commercial Museum were designed by the Hewitt Brothers, they followed the same industrial model. By the 1930s, the demand for a civic auditorium resulted in the demolition of two of the Civic Museum buildings for the new Convention Center. Designed by the politically connected city architect, Philip Johnson, its exterior is classical in detail but its construction again followed industrial models. Here the model is the great steel-arched train sheds of railroad terminals that made it possible to seat immense crowds in a clear span space. Another of the Commercial Museum halls was demolished in 2001 for the expansion of the medical center.

By the 1950s, the Medical Center had become the densest zone of the campus. In the 1970s, federal programs led to the clustering of other medical institutions in the area where they could share facilities. This brought the Children's Hospital of Philadelphia (CHOP) to its present Civic Center Boulevard location. The congestion of the site was only relieved when the city decided to close Philadelphia General Hospital. Its campus became available for the Philadelphia Center for Health Care Sciences, which houses research and hospital facilities that serve the prime tenants of the region. During the last twenty years, this too has been filled to overflowing. Once again, the dance of behemoth institutions has worked in the university's favor. After the construction of the city's new Pennsylvania Convention Center at 12th Street, the city's early twentieth-century convention center on the far side of Civic Center Boulevard has become available for twenty-first-century expansion.

*Dormitory Quadrangles, looking northwest*

## 49. Dormitory Quadrangles, "The Quad"

*Cope and Stewardson, 1894–1912; Stewardson and Page, 1912–1929;*
*Trautwein and Howard, 1945–1959*

Penn's first dormitories in nearly a century formed the centerpiece of
Provost Charles Harrison's building program. They were planned as a series
of connected quadrangles composed of small houses with rooms off internal stairs, mirroring the dormitories of Oxford and Cambridge colleges. They
were intended to eventually house the majority of undergraduates, giving
Penn the type of collegiate life that flourished on other ancient American
campuses. Just before construction got under way, John Stewardson cabled
home from England suggesting that the university adopt the brick and stone
of St. John's College, Cambridge, instead of the proposed schist and limestone that the architects had used with such effect at Bryn Mawr's Pembroke
Hall. Fortunately, Penn could use the stone already ordered for the base-
ments, and the work began on the Cambridge model for the so-called "Little
Quad" and "Upper Quad" in the triangular portion of the site at the west
end. The splendid cluster of ogee-dome capped towers of the Memorial
Tower gateway of the Upper Quad at 36th Street was completed in time to
memorialize Penn's losses in the Spanish American War.

OPPOSITE: *Memorial Tower*

TOP: *Class of 1873 Gate*
BOTTOM: *Dormitory Quadrangles*

Harrison pushed his project steadily east. In 1908 as he neared the end of his years of university leadership, his wife was able to give him the "Birthday House" as a surprise present. Two years later, Provost's Tower was given to celebrate his last year as provost. Though both Cope and Stewardson had died, Stewardson by drowning in an ice-skating accident in 1896 and Cope of a stroke in 1902, the successor firm, Stewardson and Page, continued the scheme. It modified detail toward progressively later phases of English Gothic, as if the project had unfolded over centuries rather than decades. By 1928 under the direction of George Page, flamboyant early Renaissance detail was apparent in the portals of the "Baby Quad." Even though chapel and dining halls and a third great gateway to Hamilton Walk that are depicted in the original perspective were never built, the complex holds its own among the great collegiate buildings of the world.

Few campus buildings more perfectly capture turn-of-the-century undergraduate life than the Quad. Its raised platforms were conceived as the setting from which upper classmen could watch the annual battles between freshmen and sophomores. The building's halo of carved bosses (incorrectly termed gargoyles by many) recalls the tradition of undergradu-ate caricature that survives in the school newspaper and on the walls of the Mask and Wig Club. These include owlish faculty members, donkey-eared undergraduates, and the architects as fools selling apples on the north facade. At the end of the twentieth century, the Quad's three major divisions were adapted as three college houses—Spruce, Ware, and Woodland—marking the ongoing evolution of Penn's undergraduate experience. The present landscape is the result of the work of Andropogon Associates Ltd. Its underlying principle of sustainable design has shaped choices of plants and uses of the space.

Within the Quad are three sculptures that capture the early twentieth-century spirit of the institution. In the archway between the Upper and Big Quads, a tiny bronze sculpture by the youthful Alexander Stirling Calder depicts an academically robed student with a football player in the uniform of the day. Entitled *Scholar and Athlete*, it embodied the themes of *Pennsylvania Stories*, written by Penn Professor of English Arthur Hobson Quinn. At the west end of the Upper Quad is Lynn Jenkins's sculpture of the seated figure of *Provost Harrison* who gazes across his proudest creation. On the crosswalk from the Memorial Tower is R. Tait McKenzie's impassioned figure of *George Whitfield*, which was commis-sioned in 1914 to celebrate the 200th anniversary of Whitfield's birth. His church, erected in 1740, later housed Franklin's Academy, forming the basis for Penn's claims of antiquity that enables Penn graduates to march ahead of Princeton graduates in academic processions.

Adjacent to the narrow west end of the Quad is the Class of 1873 Gate. This was donated twenty-five years after graduation by one of the first

*Dormitory Quadrangles*

classes to attend the West Philadelphia campus. It is the work of Frederick Mann and the architects of the Quad, Cope and Stewardson, and continues their Cambridge vocabulary. On the north side of the Quad is Stouffer College House, filling the space between Spruce Street and the former route of Woodland Avenue. Constructed in 1968–1972 from plans of Geddes, Brecher, Qualls and Cunningham, it echoes the formal, if not the stylistic, themes of its neigh-bor. Scale is controlled by emphasiz-ing the sub-units of the structural bays, which are defined by contrasting the concrete piers with the brown brick infill. Shops along the Spruce Street facade create a mixture of commerce and residence similar to that of medieval villages—reflecting Jane Jacobs's influence on urban design after the publication of *The Death and Life of Great American Cities* (1961). Stouffer carries the name of its chief donor, Vernon J. Stouffer (1923), head of Stouffer Foods Corp.

### 50. Leidy Laboratory of Biology *Cope and Stewardson, 1910–1911*

*Leidy Laboratory of Biology*

Across Hamilton Walk are the succes-sors to the Biological Department of a century ago. The Leidy Laboratory commemorates Professor of Anatomy and Director of the Graduate Department of Biology, Joseph Leidy (1823–1891), who was the preeminent American anatomist of his day. By the time that the Zoological Laboratory, as Leidy was originally called, was con-structed, the founders of the architectural firm were long dead. Its design had lost the freshness of the Quad and the sculptural energy of the project-ing wings and centerpiece of the John Morgan Building constructed nine years before. The result is a somewhat formulaic design of subtly projecting end and central blocks that relies on the familiar contrast of brick and lime-stone. Details were increasingly classical in inspiration.

*Alfred Newton Richards Medical Research Building*

## 51. Alfred Newton Richards Medical Research Building and Goddard Laboratories

*Louis I. Kahn, 1957–1960; 1961–1964*

Unlike Furness's revolutionary library that was stylistically out-of-date almost from the moment it was finished, but remained a model of functional success and influenced later library planning, Kahn's laboratory has struggled functionally from the moment it was completed but has continued to stimulate designers to the present. Constructed as modernism arrived at the universal solution of simple rectangular volumes to house almost any function, the Richards Laboratory marked a return to specificity of form to enhance and mold the work within. Kahn's spaces were sometimes limited in size, and frequently had too much natural light, causing scientists to block windows with foil and other materials. In 1961 as the first phase was completed, it was the subject of an exhibit at the Museum of Modern Art, where it was hailed by Wilder Green as "the single most consequential building" erected in the United States after World War II.

Its significance arises out of Kahn's effort to arrive at specific architectural forms from the requirements of the program, here conceived as small teams of researchers in central work areas served by auxiliary spaces. This set up Kahn's fundamental dichotomy of "served" and "servant" spaces. Glazed, unpartitioned work areas, which are carried on cantilevered, prestressed Vierendeel concrete trusses and columns, are juxtaposed against brick-clad vertical towers that contain ventilation shafts, stairs, and elevators. The diagrammatic specificity of form was enhanced by Kahn's use of red brick against the white precast concrete, which recalls the familiar Penn color scheme. With its broken, picturesque silhouette, Richards complements the setting adjacent to Cope and Stewardson's dormitories. Where modernism had all too often made a point of conflicting with its setting, Kahn's building brilliantly fit into Hamilton Walk. Context became a watchword for the circle of architects who worked with him on the faculty of Penn's Graduate School of Fine Arts. The core ideas of the Richards Building have been adopted by many later buildings across the campus and around the world.

The first portion of the building was named for Professor of Pharmacology and Vice President of the university for Medical Affairs, Alfred Newton Richards, M.D. During World War II, he was instrumental in the large-scale production of penicillin and was a principal developer of sulfa drugs. To the west is the second phase of the building, housing the biology laboratories. It continued the original scheme with simplified trusses and detailing. The laboratories bear the name of Dr. David Goddard, who led Penn's resurgence in biosciences after World War II and served as provost under President Harnwell.

Behind the Richards Building are the Biology Gardens, which were constructed in the 1890s. Designed by Professor of Botany John MacFarlane, the garden and adjacent greenhouses were intended as teaching tools but are now primarily noted for their visual charm. In 2001, plans were made to rehabilitate the garden by landscape architect Michael Lane as a part of a larger project that will add a laboratory wing to the Leidy Building by Ellenzweig Associates. Just west of Richards Laboratory is a

*Biology Gardens*

*Module VII, Leers Weinzapfel Associates*

modest laboratory for cell behavior, the Florence and David Kaplan Memorial Wing of the biology program. It was designed by Kahn in 1959–1960 and was enlarged with an upper story by two followers of Kahn, Thomas Vreeland and Frank Schlesinger, in 1963. It bears the name of the Philadelphia founder of the Penn Fruit Company, which pioneered the super-supermarket in Philadelphia in the 1950s. Carlos Vallhonrat designed the Seely G. Mudd Biological Research Laboratory to the rear of Leidy Laboratory in 1984–1986, with Francis, Cauffman, Wilkinson and Pepper. Its palette of dark red brick with light-toned horizontal accents recalls Kahn's Richards Laboratory, but the materials are merely a descriptive metaphor for structure rather than the structure itself.

The campus continues along University Avenue toward the river. At the link to the Schuylkill Expressway is Module VII, the Central Chiller Plant. Its glistening, stainless steel grill shimmers in the daylight and at night reveals the brilliantly lighted, boldly colored pipes and machinery behind the screen. Designed by Leers Weinzapfel Associates of Boston and completed in 2000, it carries on the tradition of esthetic engagement begun by the power plants of the Wilson Brothers and continued by Thomas, Martin and Kirkpatrick.

## 52. John Morgan Building *Cope and Stewardson, 1902–1904*

*John Morgan Building*

The nation's first medical school was founded as a part of the College of Philadelphia in 1765 by two Philadelphia graduates of the University of Edinburgh, William Shippen and John Morgan, in whose honor the building is named. It was built as part of Harrison's second phase of campus expansion. This began in 1900 with the new Law School building and was followed by the construction of immense laboratory and classroom buildings for medicine, engineering, and, in 1906, veterinary medicine, whose site was taken by the Morgan Building. In contrast to their design of the Quad, which reflected English collegiate sources in form and detail, Cope and Stewardson here worked within the rationale of modern steel-frame and structural terra-cotta construction systems. This determined the loft-like floors, which are overlaid with the campus brick and limestone vocabulary. Quoins, stringcourses, balustraded parapets, and stone-mullioned windows derived from late-seventeenth-century English public buildings accent the immense construction. Projecting wings and the elaboration of the central entrance pavilion give the main facade a three-dimensional richness that is lacking in the nearby and slightly later Leidy Laboratory. Most noteworthy is the subtly detailed central tower with its delicate appliqué of pilasters that accurately capture the mid-seventeenth-century English use of classical elements as ornament instead of structure. The marble-clad corridors and the principal stairwell within were originally brightened with deep-red upper walls and yellow and tan cornices. Behind the screen of ornament was an industrial workplace with interior light wells providing north light for the laboratories behind the glazed walls.

In 1928, Stewardson and Page enlarged Morgan with the Anatomy-Chemistry Wing at the rear. The new labs, half of whose cost was borne by the Rockefeller Foundation, were attached at the rear of the building and are slightly simpler in detail. The building contains important mementos of the school's history, including Thomas Eakins's group portrait, *The Agnew Clinic* (1889), depicting Dr. D. Hayes Agnew, the celebrated surgeon who brought asepsis to Penn's operating theaters. In the foreground, is his youthful, dark-haired assistant, Dr. J. William White, who succeeded Agnew as the chief of Penn's surgery program.

LEFT: *Robert Wood Johnson Pavilion*
RIGHT: *Edward Stemmler Hall*

## 53. Robert Wood Johnson Pavilion and
## Edward Stemmler Hall

**Robert Wood Johnson Pavilion**

*Ewing, Cole, Erdman and Eubank Architects, 1965–1969*

**Edward Stemmler Hall** *Geddes, Brecher, Qualls and Cunningham, 1976–1978*

The Johnson Pavilion is the core facility of the Medical School containing libraries, classrooms, and offices. Its design forms a transition between the Morgan Building and the now demolished Victorian hospital structures further to the east. The architects used Flemish bond brickwork, subtle belt courses of recessed brick at the sill lines, and a mansard-like parapet that caps the building.

Medical education continues into the center of the hospital complex with Edward Stemmler Hall. It was built in 1976–1978 from plans of Geddes, Brecher, Qualls and Cunningham, who monopolized much of the scientific and medical design for the university in the 1960s and 1970s. Its principal image is a finned concrete structural sunscreen wall that contrasts with Kahn's contextual design at the Richards Hall. It has the merit of reducing solar loading in response to the energy crisis of the 1970s. The building bridges Hamilton Walk as it enters the hospital core, framing a view of the colorful sculpture and pyramidal pavilion of the MRI center, which enliven a courtyard within the hospital.

## 54. Hospital of the University Of Pennsylvania

**J. William White Memorial Building**

> *Arthur H. Brockie (Arch. 1895) and Theodore M. Hastings, 1913*

**Crothers Dulles Hospital and D. Hayes Agnew Memorial Pavilion**

> *Marmaduke Tilden, H. Bartol Register (1910, Arch. 1914), and George W. Pepper (1916, Arch. 1919), 1939–1941*

**Thomas Sovereign Gates Memorial Pavilion**

> *Schmidt, Garden, and Erikson (Arch. 1910), 1950*

**Martin Maloney Memorial Pavilion** *Tilden, Register, and Pepper, 1928–1929*

**S. Ravdin Institute** *Schmidt, Garden, and Erikson, 1958 and 1963*

**Silverstein Pavilion** *Geddes, Brecher, Qualls and Cunningham, 1976–1978*

**Penn Tower** *Geddes, Brecher, Qualls and Cunningham, 1972–1974*

**Jonathan Evans Rhoads Pavilion**

> *Robert Lynn Associates in association with Payette Associates*

**David Devons Medical Imaging Center**

> *GBQC Architects (the later name of Geddes, Brecher, Qualls and Cunningham), 1985*

The zone south of Spruce Street between 34th and 36th streets is entirely occupied by the Hospital of the University of Pennsylvania—the first teaching hospital built by an American university. The initial building, designed by Thomas Richards in the academic Gothic garb of College Hall, faced Spruce Street. Later, Victorian additions were added to the east and west. All of the nineteenth-century portions have been demolished.

The earliest surviving building is the J. William White Memorial Building at the corner of 34th and Spruce streets, which was constructed

*Crothers Dulles Hospital and Thomas Sovereign Gates Memorial Pavilion*

*Thomas Sovereign Gates
Memorial Pavilion*

beginning in 1913 from plans of Arthur H. Brockie (Arch. 1895) and Theodore M. Hastings. This was to be the first phase of an immense structure that would harmonize with the Cope and Stewardson campus and would eventually replace all of the earlier buildings west to 36th Street. Though its broad wall surfaces owe much to the Georgian revival, its detail is part of the generally Jacobean flavor of the campus. This is particularly evident in the strap work of the now closed entrance on 36th Street, the projecting pedimented balcony of the sixth story, and the vestigial towers of the facade. Within were the new surgical suites of the university, accounting for its being named for J. William White, M. D., Penn's early twentieth-century chief of surgery.

The Crothers Dulles Hospital and D. Hayes Agnew Memorial Pavilion were built between 1939 and 1941 from designs of Marmaduke Tilden; H. Bartol Register; and George W. Pepper, who had designed the spirited art deco Maloney Wing at 36th Street in 1929. Here, because of its proximity to the White Building, they adopted with but little conviction Jacobean references in the palette of materials and the projecting oriels of the wings. The top two stories above the main cornice are recent additions, which display the same spiritless manner as the original. Continuing the medical division's policy of naming buildings for leading members of its faculty, Agnew is named for the brilliant nineteenth-century surgeon who is commemorated in the Eakins masterpiece that hangs in the Morgan Building; the Dulles wing commemorates a law graduate who died in the 1912 wreck of the Titanic.

The largest building of the group is the Thomas Sovereign Gates Memorial Pavilion, which was built in 1950 from plans by the early Chicago modernists and later hospital specialists, Schmidt, Garden, and Erikson. It was the first outside firm to work for the hospital in its history, but they adhered to the outline of the Brockie and Hastings project. Instead of entirely replacing the Victorian hospital buildings, they retained the rear wings and fronted them with a vast modern slab. This they overlaid with oriels and linked windows that would have succeeded in relating to the earlier buildings were it not for the color shift toward a pinkish brick. The building bears the name of financier Thomas Sovereign Gates, (1893, Law 1898)

LEFT: *Martin Maloney Memorial Pavilion*
RIGHT: *Penn Tower*

who served as president of the university and later as chairman of its board
of trustees. Gates envisioned the transformation of the hospital to the
"Philadelphia Medical Center." His bust, by Evelyn Longman Batchelder
(1941, installed 1964), is set in a small niche in the center of the vast facade.

The last building of the Spruce Street front is the Martin Maloney
Memorial Pavilion at the corner of 36th Street. It was constructed in
1928–1929 by Tilden, Register, and Pepper, who in the 1920s were among
the city's most successful modernists. In their design for the pavilion, they
adapted the verticality of the commercial art deco style to the familiar
palette of materials of the campus. The result is an avowedly modern
design that represents the shift of medicine toward technology. This is the
first building of the hospital complex named for a donor, Martin Maloney,
an Irish immigrant who made his fortune in the electrification of the city.

When the Spruce Street front was filled with hospital buildings,
additional structures were built to the south along 34th Street. The first was
the I. S. Ravdin Institute, which was erected between 1958 and 1963—once
again from designs of Schmidt, Garden, and Erikson. By that date, Penn's
planning was firmly under the control of Dean Perkins, and historical references were no longer desired. The building presents a minimalist facade of
steel-framed windows in a brick wall. Only a tiny limestone band recalls the

OPPOSITE: *Jonathan Evans Rhoads Pavilion*

*Silverstein, Ravdin, and White Pavilions*

historic color scheme of the campus. The post-modern entrance portico and lobby of 1997 were among the last projects of the Architects Collaborative of Cambridge, founded by Walter Gropius. Dr. Isador S. Ravdin, Harrison Professor of Surgery, was commissioned a general during World War II and led the Pennsylvania medical contingent in South Asia to an unprecedented reduction of mortality. After the war, he served as President Eisenhower's personal physician.

Adjacent is the starkly modern Silverstein Pavilion of 1976–1978 by Geddes, Brecher, Qualls and Cunningham. In the manner of the Philadelphia School, it differentiates patients' rooms on the upper levels from offices and the main emergency room on the base. Its sleek tan skin, on the other hand, places the architects more in the anti-contextual school of Euro-modern. Silverstein is attached by a bridge to another Geddes, Brecher, Qualls and Cunningham project, the Penn Tower, which was con-structed as a Hilton Hotel in 1972–1974 to house the expected crowds for the celebration of the nation's bicentennial. Acquired by the hospital a gen-eration ago, it now houses outpatient facilities and offices. Robert Geddes's roots in the modernism taught by Walter Gropius at Harvard are evident in the minimalist white volume that differentiates between guest rooms and vertical circulation of elevators and stairs.

Recent building activity has occurred along 36th Street and at the rear of the hospital complex. The Jonathan Evans Rhoads Pavilion occu-pies the corner at Hamilton Walk. The post-modern construction combines references to the adjacent Maloney Pavilion in its glitzy art deco motifs with allusions to the overall hospital in its palette of materials. Designed by Robert Lynn Associates in association with laboratory architects Payette Associates in 1993, it houses laboratories and patient rooms and honors Dr. Rhoads, who served on the surgical staff for more than half a century and was provost during the Harnwell presidency.

Hamilton Walk continues east under the Stemmler Pavilion into a courtyard designed in 1986 by landscape architects Hanna/Olin Ltd. In the center of the plaza is *Quadrature* (1984, installed 1986), an enameled steel sculpture by fine arts faculty member Robert Engman. Reflecting Engman's interest in the boundaries between three-dimensional form and two-dimensional edges, its white and orange-brown pieces are a puzzle that would form cylinders if fit together. The red-brown enameled pyramid that dominates the plaza and forms the backdrop to Engman's sculpture is the David Devons Medical Imaging Center. The last bit of space within the hospital complex is filled by the vast Founders Wing (with a capacity of 220 beds and an operating theater), which occupies the site of the main wing of Thomas Richards's original hospital. Built in 1985 from the design of GBQC Architects (the later name of Geddes, Brecher, Qualls and Cunningham), it is of white concrete with red tile insets. Its reversal of the proportional relationship of Penn's color scheme brightens the interior courtyard.

*Medical Education Quadrangle with Robert Engman's* Quadrature

*Gray Research Foundation for Molecular Medicine-Clinical Research Building*

### 55. Philadelphia Center for Health Care Sciences

**Center for Health Care Sciences**
**Nursing Education Building** *Morton L. Fishman Associates, 1968*
**Blockley Hall** *Supowitz and Demchick, 1963*
**Consortium** *Philip Johnson, 1912*
**Seymour Gray Research Foundation for Molecular Medicine-Clinical
Research Building** *Venturi, Rauch and Scott Brown, 1988*
**Steller-Chance Laboratories**
    *Bower, Lewis and Thrower Associates, in association with Earl Walls & Associates, 1992*
**Bio-Medical Research Building II**
    *Perkins and Will & Associates with Francis, Cauffman, Foley, Hoffmann Architects,*
    *Ltd., completed in 1999*

**Children's Hospital of Philadelphia (CHOP)**
**CHOP** *Harbeson, Hough, Livingston, and Larson in association with William A. Amenta*
**Richard D. Wood Center** *Ballinger and Co, 1989*
**Children's Seashore House** *GBQC Architects, 1989*
**Leonard and Madlyn Abramson Pediatric Research Laboratories**
    *Ellenzweig Associates, 1994 and 2001*

When the Philadelphia General Hospital was closed, its site was turned over
to the Hospital of the University of Pennsylvania, the Children's Hospital,
and the neighboring Veterans Administration Hospital for expansion of their
facilities. In less than a generation, this property has been filled as well.

*Bio–Medical Research Building II*

Penn constructed the first building of
the new complex, the Seymour Gray
Research Foundation for Molecular
Medicine-Clinical Research Building—
a 1988 design by Venturi, Rauch and
Scott Brown. They rejected Kahn's
highly articulated scheme for the
Richards Building, returning instead to
the more generalized industrial loft-
like space of Penn's earlier labs, which
could accommodate changing sizes
and requirements of research teams.
The architects adapted Cope and
Stewardson's Flemish bond in a pattern of oversized red-brown and tan-
brown stretchers interspersed with
blue-black headers and accented with
a secondary staccato of hot persim-
mon orange headers. At the top is a highway-scaled seal of the university,
recalling Venturi and Scott Brown and Steve Izenour's seminal study of
automobile-based design in *Learning From Las Vegas*.

Other Penn buildings in the Health Sciences Center have taken their
cue from the Venturi contextualism of surface, but most have pushed their
buildings ever higher in response to the demands for space. In 1992, Bower,
Lewis, and Thrower Associates, in association with Earl Walls & Associates,
built Steller-Chance Laboratories on top of an existing chiller plant that was
previously designed by Bower, Lewis, and Thrower. Panels of Flemish bond
brickwork and bold limestone moldings accent this high-rise lab which jointly
honors Professor of Psychology and later Provost, Eliot Stellar, and Professor
of Biochemistry and Biophysics, Britton Chance. Bower, Lewis, and Thrower
used many of the same motifs in the parking garage of 1989 across Curie
Avenue. The most recent of Penn's medical facilities is the Bio-Medical
Research Building II designed by Perkins and Will & Associates with Francis,
Cauffman, Foley, Hoffmann Architects and completed in 1999. It is the largest
single building of the university, containing nearly ten acres of work space.

South of the hospital and fronting on Civic Center Boulevard is the
Children's Hospital of Philadelphia (CHOP), which moved to its present site
in 1974. The relocation was encouraged by federal programs that sought to
create new efficiencies by locating medical facilities where they could share
services. To ensure that the Children's Hospital kept its own identity, its
designers, Harbeson, Hough, Livingston, and Larson in association with
William A. Amenta, made no attempt to relate to the university. Instead, they
adopted a brutalist mode of dark metal-clad offices, patient rooms, and

*Children's Hospital of Philadelphia*

other functions interrupted by monumental circulation towers clad in industrial tile. The vast bulk surrounds a skylit interior atrium, which includes a children's play area and a McDonald's restaurant. Its moderation of light and temperature is a creative response to the energy crisis of the previous year. In 2001, CHOP announced plans to expand its facilities and to redesign its central building, using the image-building architecture of Kohn Pedersen Fox of New York. They have proposed to wrap the original building in a new skin while adding a curved glass-covered wing to the south side.

The arrival of the Children's Hospital adjacent to the Hospital of the University of Pennsylvania and Philadelphia General Hospital laid the basis for the Philadelphia Center for Health Care Sciences. The wedge-shaped Tri-institutional Nursing Education Building at the rear of Children's Hospital, now called the Nursing Education Building, is an earlier response to federally sponsored consolidation. Designed in 1968 by Morton L. Fishman Associates, it housed nursing education for the three hospitals. Another survivor from Philadelphia General Hospital is the dormitory for the nursing school—a high-rise building of yellow brick and cast stone. It was designed in 1963 by Supowitz and Demchick, graduates of Penn's architecture school in its heyday under Cret. It was renamed Blockley Hall to recall the Blockley Almshouse, which provided the open space on which the university and the hospitals stand.

Children's Hospital has been building as well. Its first expansion was the Richard D. Wood Center, constructed in 1989 from plans by Ballinger and Co. That firm has long been known for industrial designs, but

*Leonard and Madlyn Abramson Pediatric Research Laboratories*

here adapts to the post-modern age in a brightly colored design that relates in scale and color to its red-toned neighbors. Philadelphia's favorite artist Sam Maitin (1951) fabricated the brilliantly colored bas-relief mural that enlivens the lobby (1991). The Richard D. Wood Center provides ambulatory patient facilities for the Children's Hospital. It celebrates the commercial genius of Wood, the descendent of an old Quaker manufacturing family who transformed his family's dairy in Wawa, Pennsylvania, into the familiar Wawa Markets. The Children's Seashore House was founded in 1872 to provide an ocean-front villa in Atlantic City for the sick children. Again, the reversal of the balance of color of its neighbors and the airy, volumetric form are hallmarks of a 1989 work by GBQC Architects. The most recent addition to the CHOP campus are the Leonard and Madlyn Abramson Pediatric Research Laboratories, which bring the blonde tones of 1990s institutional design to the medical campus. Designed by Ellenzweig Associates of Boston in 1994 and enlarged by the same firm in 2001, it is named for the founder of U.S. Healthcare, a pioneering health maintenance organization (HMO). Holding all of these disparate structures together is a handsome landscape plan by the Olin Partnership.

Along the rear of the property line stands the Consortium (a drug-rehab facility), whose colonial revival red brick, limestone quoins, window frames, and keystones reflect the mode of city architect Philip Johnson for Philadelphia General Hospital. His other contribution to the site is the splendid brick wall and iron fence that surround the complex.

# North Campus

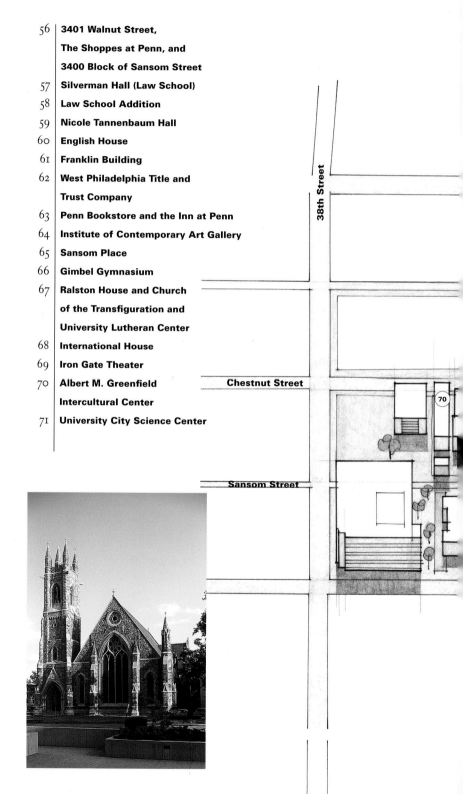

38th Street

Chestnut Street

Sansom Street

70

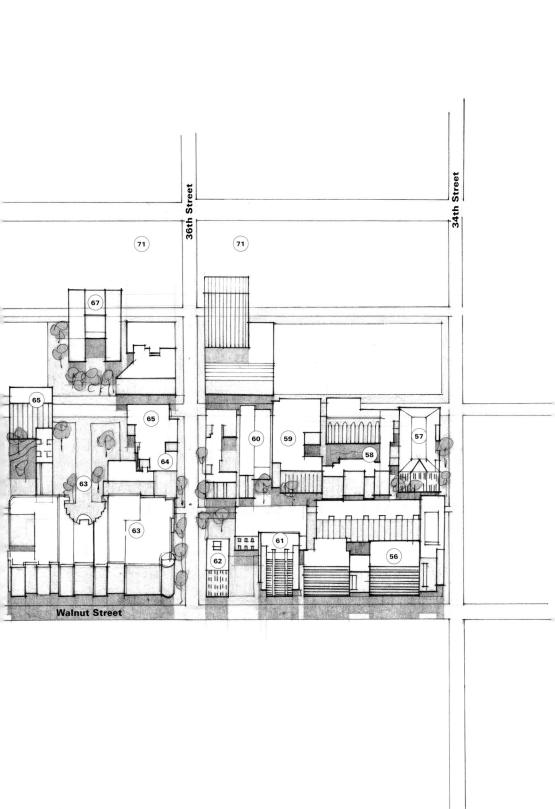

The North Campus was inaugurated with the construction of the Law School at the corner of 36th and Chestnut streets in 1899. The 1913 master plan by Paul Cret and the Olmsted firm proposed to extend the main campus to the north toward the Law School by means of a raised pedestrian crossing above Walnut Street. Those plans were never realized, and by the 1940s, the campus turned west along Locust Street. Isolated by commercial and residential rows, the Law School was an outpost of the university until the 1960s. At that time, the Redevelopment Authority condemned land for educational use between the original university campus south of Woodland Avenue to the north side of Market Street. This encouraged the large-scale synthetic planning that has typified the later campus. However, as a result of this dramatic turn of fate, the North Campus only rarely has the fine texture of the older portions of the campus.

When the university started moving west in 1872, Walnut Street became the commercial hub of the campus as row houses were converted to restaurants, bookstores, clothing stores, banks, and other businesses that catered to a transient student population. When Penn acquired its western neighborhood, it chose to concentrate retail in a pedestrian strip mall to the west at 37th Street between the central campus and the high-rise dormitories west of 38th Street that were to become the student suburb. Ironically, this re-created in miniature the urban-suburban dichotomy of 1950s highway-based planning. Land was banked in open parking lots, resulting in a stupefyingly dull landscape that seriously reduced the level of retail activity. The situation was made worse in the 1960s when the city converted Walnut and Chestnut streets into one-way viaducts to move rush-hour traffic.

At present, scattered among the new retail facilities and university offices along the north side of Walnut Street are a few survivors of the earlier commercial district. Most of the commercial structures, including Grand's Restaurant, Robert Venturi's early essay in commercial iconography, were demolished as far west as 40th Street. Present-day Walnut Street is given over to large institutional-scale buildings such as the Inn at Penn and the Gimbel Gymnasium at 37th Street; only at 38th Street does Walnut Street revert to the residential scale of the Victorian city.

The variety of scales and functions of the north side of Walnut Street contrasts with the bland institutional edge along the south side. Planned when Penn was focusing on creating a central campus spine, buildings from Van Pelt Library to the Social Sciences Complex turned their fronts away from the street, making for the most lifeless stretch of the campus. Penn has spent the better part of the last generation rectifying its earlier errors, beginning with the agreement to preserve the 3400 block of Sansom Street for shops and restaurants. This was followed by the construction of the retail base of 3401 Walnut Street and the construction of the Penn Bookstore and the shops that form the base of the Inn at Penn. Initially called "Sansom Commons," they have become a youth-oriented destination that attracts shoppers from other parts of the city.

The greatest changes in developing the north campus have occurred along Market Street, which into the 1960s was an industrial and specialty retail zone. After its condemnation by the Redevelopment Authority, the small factories and shops that provided work for the surrounding community were demolished between 33rd and 40th streets, making room for the University City Science Center. The new buildings take the form of an in-city office park, unfortunately characterized by the worst failings of redevelopment planning—a rejection of the surrounding community and a failure to provide the urban interests that would have enlivened the streetscapes. The few sculptures along Market Street do little to make up for the lack of facilities.

As the twenty-first century begins, Penn has shifted its focus to 40th Street where it has completed a monumental parking garage with a high-end grocery store at the ground floor. Its glittering stainless mesh skin enlivens the multilevel parking deck, while its contorted post-deconstructivist street facade is the most up-to-date design in the Quaker city. Fortieth Street is intended as a retail and recreation center, whose capstone will be a cinema complex of multiple screening rooms. If the directions of the present master plan hold, the North Campus will continue in its essential roles but with important changes. These will be especially apparent east of 34th Street with new housing and shopping in a converted freight terminal. The open field behind Hill College House will be transformed into a principal gateway to the university while maintaining its role as recreation space. At the west end, much depends on the future of the residential campus between 38th and 40th streets. Recent plans to weave low-rise housing and other facilities among the high-rise dormitories have been put on hold. Penn's mortgage program, the opening of the new university-supported public school, and the success of the University City Special Services District can be expected to make the region more attractive as a place for work and residence. In any event, the safe prediction is that change will remain the sole constant of the North Campus.

TOP: *3401 Walnut Street*
BOTTOM: *3400 Block of Sansom Street*

## 56. 3401 Walnut Street, The Shoppes at Penn, and 3400 Block of Sansom Street

**3401 Walnut Street** *GBQC Architects, 1985–1987*
**3400 Sansom Street** *c. 1870*

The north side of Walnut Street and the south side of Sansom Street were primarily devoted to shops and restaurants that served the student community with a frowsy insouciance that belied their position at the main entrance to the university. As the Harnwell era ended, Penn proposed to replace Elliot Cook's Moravian Café, Cy's Penn Lunch, popularly named the "Dirty Drug," the Onion, the Deck, and other student hangouts with their own shopping center. By carrying eight stories of offices above retail, parking, and movie theaters, this could be given an academic role as the "academic services building." A protracted court battle between the university and the shop owners resulted in a compromise: The houses of Sansom Street were preserved and the mass of the new building was reduced to its present five stories.

Above the street level shops, the exterior of 3401 is articulated by varied window shapes and volumes that in most Philadelphia School buildings would designate specific functions. Here they mask the universal space of conventional modernism—marking the decline into surface mannerism of the principles of Kahn and his circle that had evolved at Penn's Graduate School of Fine Arts over the previous generation. The color scheme of the exterior represents the typical GBQC reversal of Penn's red-and-white masonry. When the major surface became white limestone, small bands of red brick were too intense, resulting in a shift toward lighter tones that ended up too close to Drexel University's orange brick. The trustees were not amused! Within is a food court by David Slovic that takes its inspiration from diners. On nice days it spills out on the rear terrace, which is shared by the 3400 block of Sansom Street.

The 3400 block of Sansom Street is the best surviving example of the Victorian neighborhood into which the university moved in 1872. A brownstone Second Empire row, it housed Penn faculty and a variety of free spirits, including Mme. Helena Blavatsky, a founder of the United Order of Theosophists, who lived at 3420. In the 1960s, it became the site of the Moravian Restaurant (named for the rear Moravian Street). It was operated by Elliot Cook, a Penn architecture student and social radical who had read Jane Jacobs's *Death and Life of Great American Cities* and was prepared to act on its principles. Cook commissioned the study that caused the block to be placed on the National Register of Historic Places, eventually forcing Penn and the Redevelopment Authority to turn the block over to the business owners who had been displaced when Walnut Street was condemned. The restored block attracts students and faculty alike to a rich array of restaurants and shops.

*Silverman Hall*

### 57. Silverman Hall (Law School) *Cope and Stewardson, 1899–1900*

The chief landmark of Penn's north campus is the Law School—Cope and Stewardson's fin-de-siècle homage to Christopher Wren's garden facade of Hampton Court Palace. In 1790, James Wilson gave the first law lectures at Penn. In 1850 under Dean George Sharswood, law was taught by practicing attorneys on a per-capita basis paralleling the system of medical education. At the end of the nineteenth century, the system was reformed by William Draper Lewis (Law 1891) who as dean turned the school toward a full-time faculty. He shifted from lectures to the case study method, and brought the law school from its site on Independence Square to the West Philadelphia campus.

      The adaptation of Wren's work at Hampton Court as a source for the law school was doubly suitable. It was constructed in the red brick and light stone recently adopted by the university while also reflecting the seventeenth-century era when the modern English law code took shape. The continuity between the English and the American legal system is mirrored in the names of important justices inscribed in the rondels that cap the first-floor windows. They range from Edward I to American justices. The spectacular gated main entrance on 34th Street is once again used, and the splendid entrance hall, which has been recently restored by the firm of Shalom Baranes Associates of Washington, D.C., can be entered from the front door. Under its direction, the original mosaic floors were restored and the walls were painted a somewhat muted version of the original brilliant orange selected by Cope and Stewardson to warm up the marble-lined

*Law School Addition*

piers and grand stair. The grand stair led to the reading rooms of the Biddle Law Library, Sharswood Hall on the south, and McKean Hall on the north. After the removal of the library to Tannenbaum Hall, these great rooms have been subdivided with glazed partitions to keep a semblance of their original size. Brilliant carving in the manner of Wren's sculptor Grinling Gibbons highlights these splendid spaces.

**58. Law School Addition** *Carroll, Grisdale, and Van Alen, 1960–1962*

As evidenced by the tennis courts that formed the rear yard of the Law School, law was very much a gentlemanly profession. In 1960 the tennis courts were replaced with a dining commons, auditoria, and a library that surround a courtyard now landscaped by the Olin Partnership. The architecture took its cues from the anti-urban planning of the era, with windowless walls along Walnut Street. The cast-stone piers and segmentally arched heads nod toward the pediments of Cope and Stewardson's adjacent Law School.

TOP: *Nicole Tannenbaum Hall*
BOTTOM: *English House*

## 59. Nicole Tannenbaum Hall *Davis and Brody, 1992–1994*

The law library has been moved into Tannenbaum Hall, which now serves as the principal entrance to the Law School Complex. It follows Penn's late-twentieth-century mode of red brick laid in Flemish bond with limestone accents, but the self-conscious detail betrays the angst of 1950s modernists when adopting the post-modern mask. The symmetry of form of the main block contrasts with the asymmetrical base that carries the bulk of the historicizing detail—Flemish bond brickwork, a bull's-eye window above the entrance, and a raised parapet framing the name plaque. While these imply continuity with the main Law School building, the limestone corner piers in the main block dematerialize the facade, reiterating the modernist notion of the structural frame infilled with non-structural skin. The result of this tension can be innovative, as in the Pender Labs, or overscaled and banal, as in the law additions of the 1960s. Chaired by Penn trustee Myles Tannenbaum (Wharton School 1952), the building's name memorializes his daughter.

## 60. English House

*Schmidt, Garden, and Erikson, 1958–1960; renovations, MGA Partners, 1991*

When the nurses' quarters were demolished for the hospital's Ravdin Institute on 34th Street, this ultra-modern dormitory (named for its donor Mrs. Chancellor English) was created on the east side of the campus by the architects of the hospital's 1950s buildings. Modeled on Le Corbusier's Unités D'Habitation, the scheme places a roof deck atop a glazed slab carried on *pilotis* that framed an entrance lobby. The resulting building would have been more appropriate in a Mediterranean climate than in gritty and sometimes cold Philadelphia. In 1991, MGA Partners, successors to Mitchell/ Giurgola Associates, linked English House to King's Court, an early twentieth-century apartment house designed by Watson and Huckel, to form a larger college house. This new purpose is announced by an entrance lobby off Sansom Street. It is approached from a subgrade plaza that provides access to common rooms and a dining hall.

## 61. Franklin Building *Carroll, Grisdale, and Van Alen, 1964–1967*

In the decade of Penn's rapid expansion, the office of J. Roy Carroll (Arch. 1926), John Grisdale (Arch. 1930), and William Van Alen (Arch. 1937) regularly received commissions from Pennsylvania's General State Authority. Awarded more on the basis of work produced on time and on budget than on architectural distinction, GSA projects rarely transcended the pedestrian. This is evidenced by the Franklin Building, a cruciform tower that houses

LEFT: *Franklin Building*
RIGHT: *West Philadelphia Title and Trust Company*

Penn's central management. There are hints of Kahn's Richards Building in the placement of the columns, and perhaps a glimmer of industrial forms in the mechanical space with hoist on the top story, but the economical interior is the defining image.

## 62. West Philadelphia Title and Trust Company

*Paul A. Davis, Matthew E. Dunlap, and W. Pope Barney, 1925 and 1927*

The sole survivor of the early twentieth-century commercial strip along Walnut Street is this mini-skyscraper. Its massing owes much to Price and McLanahan's Traymore Hotel in Atlantic City of the previous decade, while its detail reflects Paul Cret's exploration of modern classicism in the 1920s. The main facade is articulated by piers that break through the parapet. The street-level banking room is marked by pilasters and roundels that linked progressive modernism to the classical tradition of bank architecture. The architectural sculptures were by Joseph Bass, a local carver. The lead architect Paul Davis (Arch. 1894) was one of those responsible for bringing Paul Cret to teach at the university, while Barney (1912, Arch. 1913) was a pupil of Cret.

*University Bookstore*

## 63. Penn Bookstore and the Inn at Penn

*Elkus/Manfredi, Architects, Ltd. 1996–1999*

When it was decided to restore Houston Hall and Irvine Auditorium for the Perelman Quadrangle instead of building a new student union, the entire block between 36th and 37th streets along Walnut Street became available for a large project. In order to attract residents to the university region, Penn's leadership proposed a mixed-use building that would make the university an appealing destination. It would incorporate the university's bookstore and a variety of shops and restaurants with an on-campus hotel. Its Boston-based designers were familiar with contextual retail infill and readily adapted Penn's color scheme to clad the immense building. Its three fronts are differentiated according to purpose; the corner tower entrance at 36th Street gives access into the bookstore, while a north-facing court provides the main entrance for hotel guests. The understated Walnut Street entrance is the main access from the campus. It leads via a gracious mission-style lobby to the faculty club, which has been incorporated into the second floor of the building. The tasteful teacup hanging from the Walnut Street facade above the entrance to the restaurant recalls Robert Venturi's non-tasteful sign for Grand's Restaurant on the same site.

TOP: *The Inn at Penn*
BOTTOM: *Institute of Contemporary Art Gallery*

## 64. Institute of Contemporary Art Gallery

*Adèle Naudé Santos and Jacobs/Wyper Architects, associated architects, 1990–1991*

Penn's avant-garde gallery was formed in 1963 by Dean G. Holmes Perkins of the School of Fine Arts as a counter to the conservative taste of the Philadelphia art world. Its first quarters in the Frank Furness–designed University Library were the scene of one of the first Warhol happenings, as well as groundbreaking exhibits on such modernists as Clifford Still. Its second home was in the central lobby of Meyerson Hall, from which it departed in 1991. Its present home is squeezed up against the south wall of the Graduate Towers. Designed by the former head of the Department of Architecture, Adèle Santos, it is a whimsical mixture of the motifs and materials of half a century of modern design to express the purposes of its program and to "intensify concern for and enlarge understanding of current thinking of this field within the university and the community at large." Ironically, this small building has more presence than the larger building that surrounds it. Its clear expression of entrance, circulation, and gallery space make it a worthy successor to the Furness tradition.

## 65. Sansom Place (Graduate Towers)

*Richard and Dion Neutra with Bellante, Clauss, Miller, and Nolan, collaborating architects, 1970*

*Sansom Place*

Beginning with Saarinen's Hill House, Dean Perkins led Penn to systematically collect the work of important modern architects for campus projects—a tradition that continues to the present. For the design of the new housing for Penn's rapidly growing graduate community, Richard and Dion Neutra were selected. They were among the Europeans who brought international modernism to the United States in the 1920s. In their bold simplicity and rugged materials, these buildings are throwbacks to the heroic age of modernism, reveling in their height against the surrounding buildings. They celebrate the transparency of modern construction, particularly in the glazed corridors that link the freestanding elevator towers serving the paired slabs.

LEFT: *Gimbel Gymnasium*
RIGHT: *David S. Pottruck Health and Fitness Center, Richard Dattner & Partners*

With the construction of the Inn at Penn to the south, the garage and raised plaza that once linked the buildings have been replaced by a landscaped drive that serves as the main entrance to the hotel. It was designed by Elkus/Manfredi Architects as a part of the inn project. The eastern towers have been renamed Nichols House in honor of Professor of History Jeanette Nichols and her husband, Professor of History and later Dean of the Graduate School of Arts and Sciences, Roy Nichols.

### 66. Gimbel Gymnasium  *Stewart, Noble, Class and Partners, 1966*

West of Sansom Place and Sansom Common is the Bernard F. Gimbel Gymnasium, constructed by the successors to Sydney Martin's office. Its location on the west side of the campus, far from the main athletic campus, was intended to serve the nearby student-housing district that was being planned. The building is named for Bernard F. Gimbel (1907), the grandson of the founder of Gimbel Brothers Department Stores and a Penn wrestler, heavyweight boxing champion, and football player. The rough-textured brick facade alludes to Saarinen's Hill House, but instead of referring to a Gothic castle, the shallow gable facing Walnut Street and the massive piers along 37th Street have more of the Greek temple in their origins. The interior houses a gymnasium and Penn's swimming pool for competition. As the guide goes to press, the gymnasium complex is being redesigned by New York architect Richard Dattner & Partners to provide space for personal fitness and has been redesignated as the David S. Pottruck Health and Fitness Center. The new addition replaces a small gallery of sporting related sculptures with multiple stories of workout space that project forward one above the other. The glazed galleria that links the addition to the original building adds a festive note like the entrance to a shopping mall.

*Church of the Transfiguration and University Lutheran Center*

## 67. Ralston House and Church of the Transfiguration and University Lutheran Center

**Ralston House**  *Wilson Brothers, 1889*

**Church of the Transfiguration and University Lutheran Center**
   *Pietro Belluschi in association with Alexander Ewing and Associates, 1969*

North of Sansom Street are buildings that once housed institutions that served the Victorian community into which Penn moved in the 1870s. The university has now acquired many, and the others generally serve the university community. The Ralston House is among these mixed-use structures, now serving its traditional role as a retirement home while also meeting community geriatric medical needs managed by the University Health System. The main building is an 1889 work by the Wilson Brothers, who dignified old age with fireplaces in every room. An adjacent modern wing was constructed in 1980 from designs of Lee and Thaete. It is now operated by Pennsylvania-Presbyterian Hospital for geriatric housing and medical offices.

   Sharing the same block is the modest Church of the Transfiguration and University Lutheran Center. Designed in 1969 by Pietro Belluschi in association with Alexander Ewing and Associates, it is shorn of the traditional detail of churches. The Greek cross plan manages to focus on both the congregants and the service. The church offices are in a separate, smaller block to the rear, recalling the similar distinction of functions in Frank Lloyd Wright's Unitarian Unity Chapel.

*International House*

### 68. International House *Bower and Fradley, 1968–1970*

Operated by a private foundation whose purpose was to find housing for international students, International House is very much a part of its community. Its design is the result of a competition that was shaped by the idea of making a building that would encourage interaction and, in the process, facilitate the creation of a community. To the surprise of the judges of the competition, the youngest architect, John Bower (Arch. 1953), was the victor. Bower taught at the university for many years. He joined the Kahn-led dialogue about community and its expression that became a hallmark of such Philadelphia School dormitories as Kahn's Erdman Hall at Bryn Mawr College. The stepped facade differentiates the functions of dormitory, meeting rooms, and communal areas in a reinforced concrete frame that refers to Le Corbusier's several Unités d'Habitation, but the enclosed shopping street and the communal spaces of the upper levels mark the architects' commitment to the goals of the program.

### 69. Iron Gate Theater (formerly the Tabernacle Presbyterian Church) *Theophilus P. Chandler, 1883–1886*

The Iron Gate Theater was built as a Presbyterian Church serving the wealthy West Philadelphia community. Of the Victorian Philadelphia architects, Boston-born and Harvard-trained Chandler most closely adhered to historical models in the years dominated by Frank Furness after the Centennial. When

*Iron Gate Theater*

taste shifted toward historical revival, Chandler was selected as dean of the reformed architecture program during its first year (1890–1891). Tabernacle is more eclectic than it seems at first glance. English and French details are mixed in a seamless homage to the ecclesiastical architecture of the middle ages that has been adapted to lusty late-nineteenth-century protestant worship of massed choirs and vast congregations. In 1890, Chandler designed the rear school and office wing screened behind a bit of cloister arcading; it now houses the university's Christian Association.

## 70. Albert M. Greenfield Intercultural Center

*Cecil Baker and Associates, 1978*

The Albert M. Greenfield Intercultural Center occupies perhaps the oldest building of the region after William Hamilton's Woodlands. Built as a Greek revival cottage well before the Civil War, its modest scale describes the suburban community that grew up before horse-cars linked Hamilton's village to the city. Real estate mogul Albert M Greenfield's gift was adapted to its new role as intercultural center by Cecil Baker and Associates as the university's response to the 1978 takeover of the Franklin Building by the Black Students League.

*Albert M. Greenfield Intercultural Center*

## 71. University City Science Center

**This is a part of campus with some twenty buildings developed to encourage scientific research and largely operated by Penn.**

**3401 Market Street** *Clarence Wunder, 1922*
**Institute for Scientific Information (ISI)** *Venturi, Rauch and Scott Brown, 1978*
**National Board of Medical Examiners** *GBQC Architects, 1993*
**Port of Technology Building** *Ueland Junker McCauley Nicholson, 2000*

*3401 Market Street*

The Science Center was a new enterprise run by a consortium of regional higher education institutions including neighboring Penn, Drexel, and Lehigh Universities, Bryn Mawr College, and Thomas Jefferson Medical School (now University).

At the core of the University City Science Center was the possibility of sharing time on the then fabulously expensive main frame computer of the university. The zone along Market Street was condemned by the Redevelopment Authority and its development was turned over to a consortium of regional colleges and universities led by Penn. The master plan provided for twenty-story office towers at the corners of the blocks that would project forward and frame low-rise loft-type incubator buildings that were to be set back from the street. In the intervening three

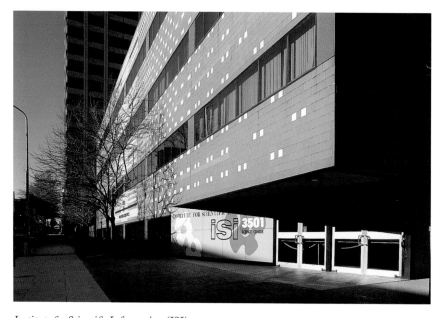

*Institute for Scientific Information (ISI)*

*Port of Technology Building*

generations, many of the low-rise buildings were constructed, beginning with 3624 Market Street and followed by 3500 and 3508. Only one tower, the so-called Gateway building at 3535 Market Street, was erected. The buildings share a tan-brown brick color (presumably intended to differ from the red and orange bricks of the two main institutional sponsors, neighboring Penn and Drexel). Ironically, as has been so often the case with modern design, plans that were conceived as big-scale and bold have proven boring and uninspired, and most of the buildings are undistinguished.

The sole surviving industrial building east of 40th Street is 3401 Market Street, which was built as the printing plant for Stephen Green and Co. in 1922. It was constructed from plans by Clarence Wunder who also designed the Hotel Pennsylvania, now Chestnut Hall. The factory shows the influence of regional proto-modernists Price and McLanahan in the expressed frame punctuated by pier-caps that articulate the roof line. Its vibration-proof concrete frame made it an ideal home for the university's first computer. Until miniaturization decentralized the computer, the information age was rooted here. To the west is Robert Venturi's 1978 high-signature, low-cost exploration of tile patterns that turned the Institute for Scientific Information (ISI) into a "decorated shed." It stimulated later Science Center architects to be a bit more adventurous, but there is more of the highway office park than the intensity of an important urban campus in this generally bland group. Together these buildings prove the virtue of Venturi's pop admonition "Less is a bore" that reversed the early modernists' "Less is more." At 38th Street, is the National Board of Medical Examiners, designed in 1993 by GBQC Architects. Yellow Minnesota dolomite—the stone that gives the warm hue to the Philadelphia Art Museum—and tinted green windows contrast with an oddly engaging mix of sci-fi and Bauhaus details. The design marks the beginning of the breakdown of the original unified palette of materials that is now evident in the recent bow fronted and silvery gray facade of the Port of Technology Building by Ueland Junker McCauley Nicholson (2000). At the rear of the National Board of Medical Examiners is a handsome, landscaped garden. Its security fence incorporates Roy Wilson's colorful *Wind Helix* sculpture.

# West Campus

Sansom Street

Walnut Street

Locust Street

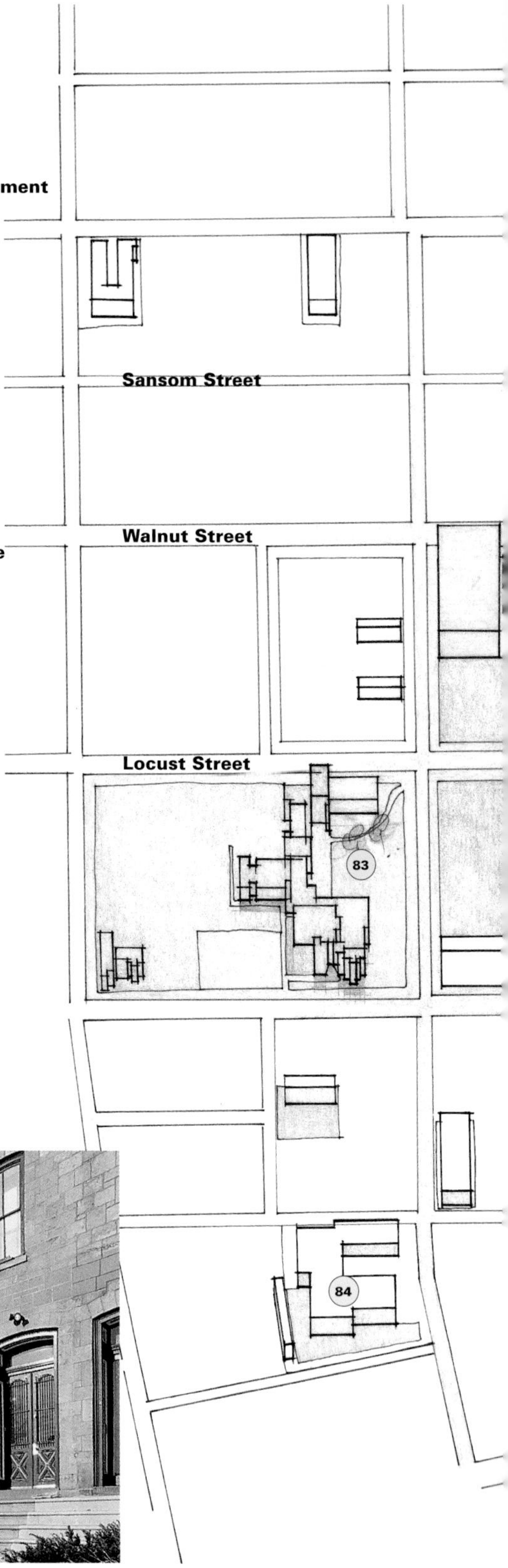

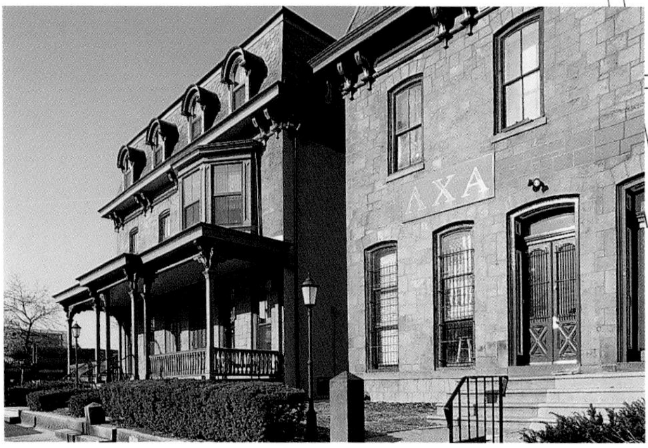

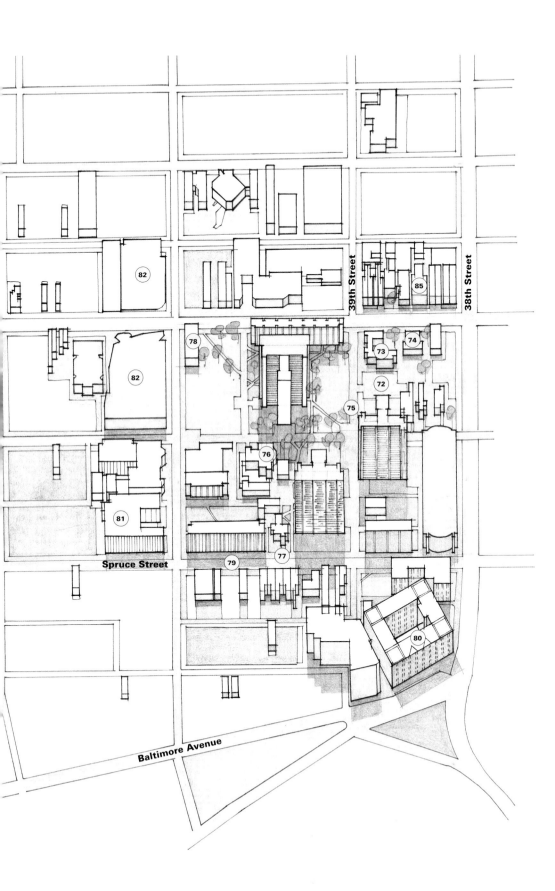

39th Street

38th Street

82

85

78

73

74

82

72

75

76

81

Spruce Street

79

77

80

Baltimore Avenue

When the construction of the Medical School pushed the Veterinary School from its site on Hamilton Walk in 1902, it was the first university building to be constructed on the far side of 38th Street. A decade later it was joined by the Dental School, which moved to 40th Street. In the same years fraternities and sororities rented or purchased houses west of 38th Street. Despite these relocations there was no concerted plan for expansion and no continuity of institutional management. Thus, it is fair to say that there was no true West Campus until the 1960s.

It was only with the 1948 plan that university leadership foresaw the transformation of 38th Street into a major north-south highway and proposed the expansion of the university across 38th Street. In that plan, the western extension was treated as a separate and distinct zone devoted to women's dormitories on the axis of Locust Street with graduate housing south of Spruce Street. If women were to be allowed on the campus, they were to be pushed as far away as possible. Graduate students were even less a part of the community, being squeezed into the blocks fronting on and south of Spruce Street.

By the 1950s and early 1960s, university planners presumed that the growth of the university would continue to be funded by state and federal grants and expansion into the neighboring community would be made possible by urban renewal programs. When the 1961 master plan was first published, it had shifted the location of student housing. Low- and mid-rise dormitory clusters for men occupied most of the four blocks between 38th and 40th streets from Spruce Street to Walnut. Women again were separated from the general community—placed this time at the Hill Hall site at 34th and Walnut streets.

By 1963, university-funded studies had determined that the new men's dormitories should follow the college house model. Detailed plans drawn by Kneedler, Mirick, and Zantzinger formed a series of diagonally placed squares of low and mid-rise buildings within the oversized super block. When Penn's 1960s development campaign did not meet its goal for funding the college houses, the university was forced to turn to the state to meet its pressing housing needs. However, state funds were insufficient to build the low-rise college house scheme, resulting in the decision to build three high-rise towers on the eastern two-thirds of the Super Block. These were served by a dining commons and a parking garage, while three low-rise dormitories were constructed on the 40th Street side of the property. This new "suburb" was linked to the main campus by a bridge over 36th Street and doubled Penn's housing capacity.

By the late 1960s, Penn had published plans that showed institutional expansion as far west as 52nd Street. This produced rising consternation among the neighboring community. Simultaneously, Penn encouraged its faculty and staff to live in the newly renamed University City, but it had not been able to affect the local school system. As a result, few new residents joined the community. Long-term residents particularly feared destabilization of the region as houses were adapted to serve as student apartments; however, the transient community of graduates and undergraduates that resulted proved to be lucrative to speculators in student housing. Coinciding with the anti-war and anti-establishment tenor of the times, tensions rose between the university and its neighbors.

With the changing demographics of the neighborhood around the university, regional retail changed as well. Long-established shops lost their sites to redevelopment. Many of these were not included in plans made by the university and its private partners for pedestrian strip malls. The result was a steady deterioration in the quality of life that saw the few faculty members who had moved into the university neighborhood departing for the suburbs. Retail declined toward the lowest common denominator. By the early 1990s, even the student population was falling as more and more chose to live in center city and dormitory rooms went unrented.

In the 1990s under President Rodin (1966), the university again focused its attention on the importance of its setting by fostering a multi-faceted assault on the issues of the region. Beginning with a general upgrading of retail, the administration sought to enhance street life while again encouraging its staff and faculty to become a part of the community. A University City Special Services District funded by the university and its institutional neighbors has restored a sense of optimism. The university's project to adapt the historic Divinity School site at 42nd Street to a university-assisted public school offers long-term hope for the future. Because Penn's future must inevitably be tied to the success of its neighborhood, the university has become a partner in the region's continuing evolution.

# 72. The Victorian Survivors in the West Campus

**Kappa Alpha Society**  *Samuel Sloan, 1851*
**Kelly Writers House**  *Samuel Sloan, 1851, redesign Harris Steinberg*
**Sigma Chi**  *T. Roney Williamson, 1884*
**Alpha Tau Omega**  *Wilson Brothers, 1891*

Penn's West Campus is most readily reached by a bridge that carries Locust Walk across 38th Street. The northeast quarter of Super Block retains much of its historic character as a part of the elite suburb that developed when horse-car lines crossed the Schuylkill and reached 42nd Street in the 1850s. Fronting on Locust Walk are two cottages built by developer S. A. Harrison in 1851 that predate the trolleys and mark the first phase of suburbanization. Designed by Samuel Sloan and published in *The Model Architect* in 1851, they have weathered a century and a half of changing tastes with their Gothic details largely intact. The easternmost cottage has long been the

TOP LEFT: *Kappa Alpha Society*
TOP RIGHT: *Kelly Writers House*
BOTTOM AND OPPOSITE: *Alpha Tau Omega*

home of the Kappa Alpha Society, while Harris Steinberg undertook the redesign of the western building, which was restored and adapted from its long-time role as the chaplain's house. It is now Kelly Writers House, a center for the encouragement of creative writing.

Next in line is the flamboyant late-Victorian, Queen Anne style mansion built as the home for Anthony Drexel, Jr.—the son of the brilliant Victorian financier who was senior partner in the firm with J. P. Morgan. Designed in 1884 by T. Roney Williamson, one of the region's more pyrotechnically inclined architects, it now houses Sigma Chi fraternity. It formed a part of the Drexel family compound, which included the patriarch's mid-nineteenth-century Italianate mansion fronting on Walnut Street and the adjacent Alpha Tau Omega house at the corner of 39th Street (the home of another Drexel son, named for Anthony Drexel's great friend George W. Childs). The more reserved manner of Alpha Tau Omega places it at the beginning of the neo-Georgian style that flourished as the nineteenth century ended. Of brick and brownstone, it is the work of the Wilson Brothers, who, while known for their engineering and planning projects, were gifted architects as well. Their firm also designed the Drexel banking house at Fifth Street (now demolished) and the main building of the Drexel Institute of Technology (now Drexel University, see Neighborhood).

### 73. Samuel Fels Center of Government

*Frank E. Newman and James R. Harris, 1907–1909*

*Samuel Fels Center of Government*

When Anthony Drexel's mid-nineteenth-century Italianate mansion was demolished at the corner of Walnut and 39th streets, it provided the site for two imposing houses for a new generation of Philadelphia's industrial elite. The first to be built was the Colonial Revival home of Samuel Fels, manufacturer of the nationally known Fels-Naptha soap. His interest in utopian communities resulted in the donation of his house to the university to foster Fels's utopian interests. The Fels Center is devoted to the training of city managers and planners. The building marks the turn toward the greater historical accuracy that prevails at the beginning of the twentieth century. Brick quoins frame the entrance and corners with a marble surround for the door. Ironically, the result owes more to Virginia than to local models.

*President's House*

## 74. President's House (originally Otto Eisenlohr House) and 3806-3808 Walnut Street

**President's House** *Horace Trumbauer, 1910–1911*
**3806-3808 Walnut Street** *W. Frisbey Smith, 1898–1899*

Whereas Fels's house was of the conventional Philadelphia red brick in the colonial revival mode, cigar manufacturer Otto Eisenlohr chose the white limestone and green slate of New York's Fifth Avenue and Newport's gilded age mansions. His French-inspired country house is presumed to have reflected the talents of Julian Abele (Arch. 1902), the first African American to graduate from Penn's architecture program. Abel had returned from the Ecole des Beaux Arts to Trumbauer's office in 1906, making his participation in the project likely. Its T-plan hallway links the front entrance to a cross hall dominated by a grand stair, making it an outstanding stage set for entertaining. Since its 1981 rehabilitation by Dagit/Saylor Architects, it has found an appropriate use as the home of the university's presidents.

The Drexel family compound remained an oasis of mansions in a region that was filling in with more modest developer's houses. Adjacent to the President's House is 3806–3808 Walnut Street, which was designed in 1898–1899 by a developer's architect, W. Frisbey Smith. Its rich pressed-metal detail on cornices and porches, and a remarkable array of balconies and other delights, demonstrate the application of mass production techniques to ornament. It now houses university offices.

## 75. Hamilton Village

*Eshbach, Pullinger, Stevens and Bruder, Associates,*
*and Perkins and Romañach, 1968–1971*

**Class of 1920 Commons** *1971, alterations by Research Planning Associates, 1986*
**W. E. B. Dubois House, Van Pelt House, and the Class of 1925 House**
**(Low Rises)** *1970*
**Harold C. Mayer Hall** *1964–1965*

*Class of 1925 House, Gregory*
*College House*

The West Campus was separated by 38th Street, which had been widened to alleviate the traffic pressures caused by closing north-south streets east to 34th Street. This led a design team headed by the Dean of the Graduate School of Fine Arts, G. Holmes Perkins, and longtime Professor of Design, Cuban-born architect Mario Romañach, to make the bold proposal to transform the scale and character of the new residential quarter along the lines of Le Corbusier's visionary "Radiant City" project for Paris in the 1920s. A reinforced concrete bridge carries Locust Walk across 38th Street, terminating in a plaza in front of the Class of 1920 Commons. The Commons and its attached garage were completed in 1971 as the final piece of the complex. It reiterates the visually unifying theme of reinforced concrete. Massive poured-in-place walls envelop skylighted dining rooms, a reference to Kahn's Erdman Hall at nearby Bryn Mawr College. Projecting stair towers and a lattice of beams and columns carrying the parking decks articulate the multiple roles of the building. The slick metal front is a 1986 addition by Research Planning Associates with Maria Romañach, daughter of the original designer.

With the exception of the northeast cluster of houses, the neighborhood and streets of four city blocks were replaced by three soaring, reinforced concrete T-plan towers. They are capped by sky-top lounges that make a virtue of their height. Each tower sits in a different position within its block: the easternmost is pushed toward the west side by the Class of 1920 Commons; the southwest tower stands closer to Spruce Street, and the northwest tower stands with its south-facing stem centered on Locust Walk. Together they are a heroic statement about the belief in technology as a force for progress. Unhappily, this Stalinist grouping has proven no more successful for undergraduate dormitories than it did for public housing. In the 1990s, the university sponsored a competition to redesign Super Block, with two winning

OPPOSITE: *Class of 1925 House*

*Harold C. Mayer Hall*

schemes. Kieran Timberlake Associates called for adding additional stories of lounges, so that each tower could be divided into three college houses and still have its own lounge; the other scheme by Patkau Associates (of Vancouver, B.C.) called for infill housing that would eliminate the open space of the original design, re-creating the missing urban fabric and streetscape. At present, both schemes are stalled, but the need for change remains.

In the 1990s, Super Block was renamed Hamilton Village. In its midst is a super-scaled sculpture entitled *Covenant*, a 1975 work by Alexander Lieberman. Brilliantly sited, it forms a triumphal arch of steel tubes that frames the westward extension of Locust Walk.

North and south of Locust Walk are the Low Rises known individually as W. E. B. Dubois House, Van Pelt House, and the Class of 1925 House. These were designed in 1970 by Eshbach, Pullinger, Stevens, and Bruder, with Perkins and Romañach as integral parts of the Super Block complex. They abandon its palette of materials and the careful siting of the high-rises for rowhouse-scale buildings in an oversized brown brick. The resulting discontinuity was intended to form a connection with the low-rise brick neighbors to the west. Comparison with the effective unity of Sert's low-, mid-, and high-rise housing for Harvard is obvious and unflattering. Each building now serves as a separate college house with different agendas.

Harold C. Mayer Hall, fronting on Spruce Street, was the first building to be constructed by the university on the new Super Block. It

OPPOSITE: *Hamilton College House with* Covenant

*Harnwell College House with Zeta Beta Tau*

bears the name of Harold Mayer (Wharton 1915), university trustee and senior partner in the Wall Street firm of BearStearns and Co. Constructed in 1964–1965 from plans by Eshbach, Pullinger, Stevens, and Bruder, it marks the first phase of an alternate scheme of simple rectangular slabs for the low-rise college house project. Fortunately, only this one portion was constructed. As originally built, Mayer Hall was slightly less drab, with blue and yellow panels below the windows. Regrettably, these were replaced in the 1980s.

Scattered among the high- and low-rises are a few bits of the earlier neighborhood. Fronting on 39th Street is Zeta Beta Tau, which was designed in 1929 by Edwin L. Rothschild (Arch. 1916), whose father was the faculty advisor. Its sleek modern Gothic in Penn's traditional palette links it to the historic campus. Set back from Locust Walk, adjacent to St. Mary's Protestant Episcopal Church is Civic House, another mid-nineteenth-century Gothic villa that was built as the church rectory. It now forms a center for campus groups that work with schools and other neighborhood institutions.

## 76. St. Mary's Protestant Episcopal Church

*Thomas W. Richards, 1871–1873*

*St. Mary's Protestant Episcopal Church*

When the Hamilton family lived at the Woodlands Mansion (see Walk Seven), they provided the site for an Episcopal church, supposedly with the requirement that they be able to see its steeple from their house. That early building is long gone as is a later successor. The present building has important links to the history of the university because it was the work of the architect of the campus buildings, Thomas Webb Richards. Built of the local schist instead of the campus serpentine, St. Mary's could appear in any Victorian suburb of London. A magnificent altar imported from Italy was installed in 1890. At the same time, the chancel was remodeled and the west porch added by the important ecclesiastical architect Charles M. Burns, whose masterpiece is the nearby Church of the Saviour (see Walk Seven). In its simple massing and roof forms, the attached school building recalls the rural-vernacular–inspired work of C. F. A. Voysey. It was added in 1897 by George Nattress, Burns's longtime assistant.

## 77. Wayne Hall *Wilson Brothers, 1876*

*Wayne Hall*

Among the most colorful designs of the Victorian neighborhood is a house facing Spruce Street that was enlarged in 1876 from plans of the Wilson Brothers for iron merchant Joseph D. Potts. Now called Wayne Hall, its strong detail and bands of colored brick and tile were unusual in domestic design and suggest the influence of Frank Furness. On the east corner, an iron solarium whose crowning glass roof has been removed was probably supplied from Potts's business. The building is now the home of WXPN, the university's award-winning radio station. At the rear, the carriage house has been adapted to serve as a center for the university's gay and lesbian community.

## 78. West Philadelphia Branch of the Free Library

*Zantzinger and Borie, 1904*

*West Philadelphia Branch
of the Free Library*

At the northwest corner of Super Block is the now vacant West Philadelphia branch of the Free Library. It was constructed in 1904–1905 on land donated by the family of Clarence Clark. Designed by two young graduates of Penn's architecture program, Clarence Clark Zantzinger (1895) and Charles L. Borie (1892), it was one of the first Carnegie libraries in the city. The facade is graced by rows of shelved books that serve as capitals above broad stylized pilasters. In the 1960s, Martin, Stewart and Noble reprised their award-winning design for the city's Mercantile Library by demolishing the north wall and replacing it with glass—a triumph of international modernism over beaux-arts subtlety. Plans are now afoot to restore the building to its historic use as a public library.

## 79. Spruce Street

**Beta Theta Pi** *Wendell and Smith, 1899, altered in 1986 by James Oleg Khruly + Associates*
**Alpha Chi Omega** *unknown, 1900*
**Sigma Alpha Epsilon** *1893, adapted by William Steele (1911), 1922*
**House of Our Own** *Willis G. Hale, 1890*
**Pi Lambda Phi** *redesigned by Andrew C. Borzner (1910)*
**Chi Omega** *W. Frisbey Smith, 1899*
**Phi Kappa Psi** *unknown, c. 1885*
**Alpha Epsilon Pi** *altered by Frank Hahn (Engineering 1900), 1922*
**Delta Kappa Epsilon**

> *Harry Sternfeld (1911, Arch. 1914, Paris Prize, and for many years a Professor of Design in the School of Fine Arts) in association with John I. Bright, 1927*

Spruce Street is now the site of several university fraternities. At the east end is Beta Theta Pi, which was built as a federal revival twin house in 1899 by the regional developers Wendell and Smith and altered in 1986 into a single fraternity by James Oleg Khruly + Associates. Its neighbor is Alpha

*Spruce Street*

Chi Omega, an early twentieth-century Tudor revival twin. It adheres to the campus Gothic style, but was built as private housing. To the west is the copper-trimmed Sigma Alpha Epsilon fraternity with overhanging roof and projecting bay; built as a residence, it was adapted to serve as a fraternity by brother William Steele in 1922. Next in line is a much-altered group of four-story townhouses by Philadelphia's unrepentant master of "More is

*House of Our Own*

More" architecture Willis Hale. Nearly art nouveau in their curvilinear detail, they represent nouveau riche taste as the nineteenth century ended. The best preserved are the alternative bookstore, A House of Our Own, and its neighbor. At the eastern end, facades have been replaced; Pi Lambda Phi was redesigned by Andrew C. Borzner in an elegant early Renaissance mode.

W. Frisbey Smith's over-the-top developer's style is evident in a pair of twin houses erected in 1899, one of which houses Chi Omega. Though some of the stamped metal has been replaced, the array of mini-balconies, ornamental bays, and pediments tells of the delight in ornament of the rising consumer culture. A tough Victorian red brick twin house with brownstone detail is home to Phi Kappa Psi. Its turned porch posts, incised brownstone lintels over the windows, and massive brick cornice show the influence of Frank Furness's vigorous reshaping of the regional post-centennial vocabulary. Alpha Epsilon Pi's house began as a mid-nineteenth century Italianate cottage. It was altered for the fraternity by Frank Hahn in 1922.

South on 39th Street and adjacent to the School of Veterinary Medicine is Delta Kappa Epsilon by Harry Sternfeld in association with John I. Bright. Designed in 1927, its handsome schist and limestone moderne Gothic style contrasts with the Veterinary School.

## 80. School of Veterinary Medicine

**Gladys Hall Rosenthal Building** *Paul Monaghan and Forrest, 1963*
**School of Veterinary Medicine** *Cope and Stewardson, 1907, 1909, 1911, and 1913*
**Small Animal Hospital** *Vincent Kling Partnership, 1978*

South of Spruce Street are the buildings of the School of Veterinary Medicine. Fronting on Spruce Street is the modest Gladys Hall Rosenthal Building, designed in 1963 by Paul Monaghan and Forrest. Its blank facade and regularly articulated side elevations recall Harbeson, Hough, Livingston, and Larson's Harrison chemistry building of a few years earlier. It is attached at its rear to another of Cope and Stewardson's hallmark red brick and

*School of Veterinary Medicine*

*Thomas W. Evans Museum and Dental Institute*

limestone-trimmed buildings—the late medieval revival quadrangle for the School of Veterinary Medicine. Opening through a broad Tudor arch into a courtyard, it was constructed one wing at a time in 1907, 1909, 1911, and 1913. The archway was scaled to its patients, which range from cows and horses to lions and dogs. At the far end of the courtyard a projecting bay marks a small lecture room. The south wing contained the hospital that is now in its new quarters. The most recent construction for the school is the Small Animal Hospital, which was designed in 1978 by the Vincent Kling Partnership. It exhibits the same muted monochromatic mode that the architects used for the contemporary Annenberg Center. Billy Lawless's brightly painted steel sculpture *Life Savers* (1982) enlivens the forecourt.

### 81. Thomas W. Evans Museum and Dental Institute (School of Dentistry)

**Thomas W. Evans Museum and Dental Institute**
  *John T. Windrim with Cope and Stewardson, consulting architects, 1912–1915*
**Shattner Center** *Bohlin, Cywinski, Jackson Architects, completed 2001*
**Leon Levy Oral Health Sciences Building (Center for Oral Health Research)**
  *Francis Cauffman Foley and Hoffmann, 1969*

The tale of Dr. Thomas W. Evans's bequest to the university reads like a melodrama; he was involved with the escape of Napoleon III's wife from Paris (she was hidden in his coach) and provided "pain-free" dental care

*Shattner Center, Bohlin, Cywinski, Jackson Architects*

for European kings and queens. His will provided that a dental institute and museum be established on the site of his former home in his native Philadelphia. This was to house his collection of art and memorabilia, much of it given by grateful artists and other clients who used Evans's services during his years of practice in Paris. Because the French courts allowed only a portion of his fortune to leave the country, it became apparent that it would be impossible to independently achieve his entire goal. His executors therefore proposed to link with the university's School of Dentistry, which quickly agreed to join the project and to move their school to new quarters at 40th and Locust streets. Instead of using Cope and Stewardson as architects, the city-dominated board chose the politically connected John T. Windrim. He proposed an H-planned building in the campus Tudor Gothic. Its principal entrance is through a towered portal into a monumental stair hall that provides access to the museum on the first level and to offices and dental clinics at the rear. The great Gothic hall is remarkable for its detail—though it probably did little to comfort patients. Where Cope and Stewardson usually managed a lyrical gentility, Windrim's mode is harsher and crisper, and there is an edge to the dental-themed grotesques that enliven the facade. In the courtyard off 40th Street is Ernest Shaw's *Shongun XII* (1983).

The School of Dentistry continues north with the Shattner Center building by Bohlin, Cywinski, Jackson, which was completed in 2001. It provides a new public entrance to the Dental School into a light-filled hall that attests to the skills of one of eastern Pennsylvania's most interesting firms. Its brick and limestone facade is derived from Windrim's Evans Building and screens the Leon Levy Oral Health Sciences Building (Center for Oral Health Research), which was constructed in 1969 from designs of Francis

Cauffman Foley and Hoffmann. Another of Penn's buildings that explore Kahn's theme of served and servant spaces, these ideas are here realized with a simpler floor plate that permits more flexible laboratories. It is named for Dr. Leon Levy, a graduate of the School of Dentistry and a frequent benefactor of school programs.

## 82. Hamilton Square

*Carlos Zapata of Wood and Zapata, 2000–2002*

North of the Dental School are two new buildings that reflect Penn's determination to make the university neighborhood retail district into a regional attraction. Towering above the intersection of 40th and Walnut streets is the just-completed Fresh Grocer, which provides a commercial corner that enlivens a gigantic parking garage. Designed by Carlos Zapata of Wood and Zapata, of Boston, its shimmering steel skin over a concrete frame and its curving colored planes are a bold contrast to the red-brick contextualism that has dominated university design for the past generation. More Tokyo than West Philadelphia, this raises the bar for regional commercial design.

Across Walnut Street, the university is building a theater complex that will bring art and limited release films to the region. It is also the work of Zapata and is conceived as a frame to Walnut Street as it leaves the university neighborhood. The design for the Cineplex takes on the curving

*Fresh Grocer*

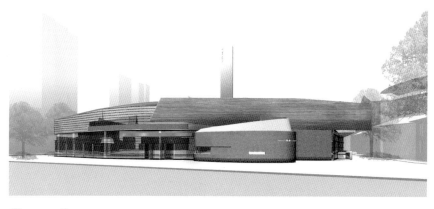

*Cinemas at Penn*

facades of 1940s movie houses, but uses modern metal screens and spiral ramps to enliven the facade. Renderings suggest that it will be the most baroque of Penn's new buildings.

### 83. University City Public School
### (formerly Philadelphia Divinity School)

*Clarence C. Zantzinger, Charles L. Borie, and Milton B. Medary 1919–1960; enlarged and adapted as public school by Atkin, Olshin, Lawson-Bell Associates in 2001*

*University City Public School, Atkin, Olshin, Lawson-Bell Associates*

In 1921 the Philadelphia Divinity School of the Protestant Episcopal Church acquired the city block formerly occupied by the estate of Clarence Clark and commissioned Zantzinger, Borie, and Medary to develop a plan for the complex. The architects, then the favored designers of elite Philadelphia, were all Penn alumni. Clarence Clark Zantzinger (1895) first formed a partnership with Charles Borie (1892); later the brilliant designer Milton Medary (who attended classes in the 1890s) joined them.

The architects' carved plaster model—now on display in the university's Architectural Archives—shows the entire site developed. The seminary and St. Andrew's Chapel are sited along 42nd Street, and the remainder of the block was to be occupied with faculty residences and dormitories in late English Gothic, of Wissahickon schist with limestone trim. Though much of the complex was never completed, the principal group with its library (1921), chapel (1924), and classrooms (1951 and 1955) is among the region's most effective high church designs. The subtle shifts in style suggest the evolution of the complex over centuries.

When the seminary merged with the Cambridge Theological Seminary, the buildings were acquired by the university and for a decade housed a neighborhood private school. The university's 1990s goal of enhancing its community led to the idea of developing the site as a university-related school. After much debate over whether it should be public or private, the decision was made to support a public school with university assistance in design and resources. Atkin Olshin Lawson-Bell's new building, though obviously modern, blends in hue and incorporates spaces of the historic buildings to create a lively setting for K–8 grades.

## 84. 4200 Pine Street (Marie Eisenlohr Residence)

*Horace Trumbauer, 1904*

The near twin to the home of the university president was built by the same architect for another member of the Eisenlohr family. It is slightly larger in scale and shifted from limestone to brick with limestone trim, but the beaux-arts flavor continues in its axial plan and bold detail. The house became the headquarters of the College of Physicians and was enlarged for that owner in the original palette of materials by William Edward Frank, the successor to Trumbauer's office. Acquired by the university, it now houses the University of Pennsylvania Press.

*4200 Pine Street*

## 85. Walnut Street West of 38th Street

**3805–15 Walnut Street** *attributed to Frank Furness's office, 1889*
**Tau Epsilon Phi, 3805–07 Walnut Street**
  *renovated by Becker/Winston Architects (Bill Becker, Arch.1972 and Richard Winston,*
  *Arch. 1972), 1992*
**Sigma Nu, 3819 Walnut Street** *pre–1873, updating Baker and Dallett, 1904*
**Lamda Chi Alpha, 3829 Walnut Street** *unknown, c. 1873*
**Sigma Delta Tau, 3833–35 Walnut Street** *unknown, c. 1873*
**The Rotunda, 4012 Walnut Street** *Carrère and Hastings, 1911*
**Sigma Phi Epsilon, 4028 Walnut Street** *Walter Smedley, 1900*
**4015 Walnut Street** *George Kingsley, 1926*

*Sigma Nu*

West of 38th Street and north of Walnut Street are numerous houses that have been adapted as fraternities and sororities. While many are minor works of architecture, they tell the story of the evolution of Penn's neighborhood from its early days as a horse-car suburb to a dense urban neighborhood in the twentieth century. Across from the president's house at 3805–15 Walnut Street are a group of much altered brick twins attributed to Frank Furness's office. Built when Furness was designing the University Library, they share some of its details and materials. They were designed as two sets of contrasting pairs; the easternmost brownstone-fronted twin has been demolished for the widening of 38th Street. Its counterpart on the west has been shorn of its detail and hidden behind a metal screen that recalls Edward Durrell Stone's treatment of his Victorian house in New York. Like the other houses in the group, 3805–07 is missing its front porch—a sculptural affair of massive turned posts with knee-braced struts that formed a gracious space before Walnut Street was turned into an automobile viaduct. Renovated by Becker/Winston Architects in 1992 as the home of Tau Epsilon Phi, it retains its original robust copper bay.

  To the west are other fraternities and sororities, including Sigma Nu, an extraordinary mid-nineteenth-century Italianate mansion. Its massive cornice and rooftop belvedere hint at the opulence of Anthony Drexel's now demolished house that used to stand on the opposite side of Walnut Street. Colonial Revival details date from a 1904 updating by Baker and Dallett.

  The twin mansarded brownstones with porch fronts at the west end of the block house Lamda Phi Epsilon and Sigma Delta Tau. Dating from the centennial-era boom in West Philadelphia, they describe the comforts of middle class life supported by the workshop of the world.

*3805–15 Walnut Street*

The West Philadelphia suburb extends west and north with a mixture of engaging, small-scale buildings that convey tired deterioration and the potential of human-scaled charm. Just west of the 40th Street gateway is the Rotunda, formerly known as the First Church of Christ Scientist, which was designed in 1911 by Carrère and Hastings, the architects of New York's Public Library and other beaux-arts landmarks. Conscious of local scale, they adapted the simple planes and details of Early Christian architecture to house a neighborhood church. Its rotunda scheme with short cross arms complicates Penn's plans for its future use. Adjacent to the First Church of Christ Scientist is Sigma Phi Epsilon, a handsome fin-de-siècle Georgian revival city house by Walter Smedley. Across Walnut Street is a multistory Greek Treasury clad with glistening tiles, whose polychromy and scale reflect the simultaneous construction of Philadelphia's golden-hued art museum. Forty-fifteen Walnut Street was built in 1926 as the Atlas Storage Company by New York architect George Kingsley. Originally, it provided a secure site for household valuables when families were away for extended periods of time. It is now the site where student editors and writers produce the *Daily Pennsylvanian*, the city's fourth-largest daily newspaper.

# Penn off Campus

Elements of Penn's campus are scattered across the city. These offer the chance to see Society Hill, one of Philadelphia's notable historic neighborhoods and the community where Penn began.

## 86. Center for Judaic Studies and Mask and Wig Club

**Center for Judaic Studies** *GBQC architects, 1992–1993*
**Mask and Wig Club** *adaptation Wilson Eyre, Jr., 1894*

*Center for Judaic Studies*

In the old city, nearly opposite Independence Square at 419 Walnut Street is the Center for Judaic Studies. Funded by Walter Annenberg and designed by GBQC architects in 1992–1993, it adopts the red brick and white stone trim of the old city in an unusually contextual post-modern design. To the west on a tiny north-south alley is the Mask and Wig Club. For more than a century, male undergraduates have manned all roles in the theatrical productions of this club. Located at 310 South Quince Street, it is a splendid arts and crafts–styled adaptive reuse by Wilson Eyre, Jr., in 1894 of a modest building that began as a Lutheran chapel and later served as a dissecting laboratory for Jefferson Medical College students.

*Mask and Wig Club*

*University of Pennsylvania Boat Club*

### 87. University of Pennsylvania Boat Club

*probably Thomas W. Richards, 1875*

On the river banks above the Philadelphia Museum of Art is the oldest surviving university athletic facility, the much-mutilated University of
Pennsylvania Boat Club. Built in 1875 of local brownstone, its Gothic detail
suggests that it was probably the work of the university's architect Thomas
W. Richards. Over the past generation, Olympians have rowed out of the
building—but the building has been functionally and crudely enlarged with
little regard for its materials or its design.

### 88. Morris Aboretum

*John and Lydia Morris, restoration Andropogon Associates, Ltd., 1978–1995*

In 1978, the University of Pennsylvania undertook its first important
restoration project at the Morris Arboretum at 100 Northwestern Avenue in
the city's Chestnut Hill neighborhood. The late-nineteenth-century creation
of John and Lydia Morris, it has been carefully and splendidly restored by
Andropogon Associates, Ltd, whose principals, Carol Franklin (Landscape
Arch. 1965), Colin Franklin (Landscape Arch. 1967), Leslie Sauer, and Rolf
Sauer (Arch. 1971) have carried the banner of sustainable design of their
teacher Ian McHarg. They rediscovered the principles of the garden design
and adapted the carriage house into a visitor's center. Recently, they
designed a new Victorian-styled fernery.

Even further removed from the university is the New Bolton Farm of the School of Veterinary Medicine in Chester County's picturesque Kennett Square. It replaced a Bucks County property, Bolton Farm, given by Effingham B. Morris, president of the Girard Estate and has much history of its own. On its grounds is the early eighteenth-century second home of Caleb Pusey, who was a partner with William Penn in the earliest mill in the commonwealth. Modern medical facilities make this a mecca for the medical care of larger animals.

Farthest of all from the heart of the campus is the university's **Penn Club** at 30 West 44th Street in Manhattan. Designed in 1900 as, dare it be said, the Yale Club by Yale graduates Tracy and Swartwout, it later housed a rabbinical school, Truro College. It was acquired in 1988 by the university to house a club for its Manhattan alumni. Fortunately, its red brick and limestone trim conform to Penn's historic palette and its location amidst the Harvard, Princeton, and New York Yacht Club buildings suits its present use. Adapted by David Helpern Architects of New York City, it incorporates university themes in a suite of public spaces. At its heart are the splendid Penn Grill Murals by Max Mason (Master of Fine Arts, 1984) that depict events of the academic year. Fall is represented by Penn's thrilling 1982 gridiron conquest of Harvard; winter depicts the campus Green under a blanket of snow, and spring provides a view of oarsmen at Penn's dock on boathouse row. Together they emphasize the role of Penn's architecture in the shared memories of the university's ever-widening community.

## Penn's Surroundings

No guide to Penn's campus would be complete without an overview of its special setting in a suburb of the city where much of the American adventure began. Scattered through the immediate vicinity are trophies of Philadelphia's rich history that are well worth a visit. Within University City are historic churches that represent the early Swedes, German Lutherans, Scots Presbyterians, Irish and European Catholics, as well as African Americans, Koreans, and others who continue to arrive in Penn's City of Brotherly Love.

Landmarks associated with Penn's founder Benjamin Franklin are principally scattered across the old city to the east along the Delaware River. They range from Venturi and Rauch's imaginative museum at the site of his house on the 300 block of Market Street to his club, which became the Library Company (now at 1320 Locust Street). The eighteenth-century buildings of Pennsylvania Hospital at 8th and Pine streets (now a part of the University of Pennsylvania's medical system) extended medical care to the

*Woodlands Mansion*

entire city; Franklin's Academy and Charitable School became the College of Philadelphia and ultimately the University of Pennsylvania, which is now Philadelphia's largest employer and its principal global enterprise.

Philadelphia's role in shaping a distinct American culture is evident in the buildings of the early university, as well as in thousands of buildings across the city that survive from the early republic.

## 90. Woodlands Mansion

One of the finest of Penn's neighbors is central to the history of Penn's present neighborhood. The Woodlands Mansion—now the central offices of the Woodlands Cemetery—is reached through a Paul Cret–designed gate at 40th and Woodland Avenue. (Cret's house was around the corner at 512 Woodland Terrace). Built as the home of William Hamilton, a member of Penn's first college class of 1757, the Woodlands incorporated an earlier structure in its 1780s enlargement. There may be no more splendid example of the architecture of the early republic than this jewel of a house. The sculptural grandeur of the riverside portico contrasts with the sophistication of the opposite pilastered facade. These differing facades are complemented by the first-floor plan of classical-derived rooms that form an interlocking suite. It is a remarkable achievement that outdoes any American house of its time. Originally stuccoed, its exposed rubble walls with brick arches and window surrounds are a twentieth-century alteration that reflected then contemporary fashion. Toward the road is a stable whose facade is deeply niched and is intended as a foil to the main house.

The grounds were once an arboretum that complemented John Bartram's nearby gardens. Acquired by a private cemetery company in the middle of the nineteenth century, the property is now dotted with grave markers and mausoleums. The Gothic spire of the Moore family is the work of John Kutts, an architect of the mid-nineteenth century. The Wilson Brothers solved the complicated foundation problems of the great obelisk that signals the burial place of Thomas Evans, donor of Penn's Dental School. Other notables are buried here, including the Drexel family in a marble mausoleum on the river side of the mansion and the brilliant designer of Penn's University Museum, Wilson Eyre, Jr., whose grave is marked by a plain marble slab that merely gives his dates and name. The cemetery grounds are open to the public seven days a week 9:00 A.M. to 5:00 P.M.

## 91. John Bartram House and Garden

*probably John Bartram, 1730, 1771*

Older than Woodlands and far more ruggedly individual is the remarkable house and garden of early American botanist John Bartram. It looks out over the Schuylkill just to the south of the Woodlands Mansion. Built in two stages in 1730 and in 1771, it is a provincial version of Georgian style. The center is dominated by a recessed two-story portico that is framed by crude

*John Bartram House*

Ionic columns (reduced to one story with plank infill at a later date). Bartram's religious independence caused him to be expelled from the Darby Friends Meeting for doubting the divinity of Jesus Christ and perhaps explains the contentious inscription on a second-story panel, "It is God Alone Almyty Lord / The Holy One by Me Adord / John Bartram 1770." Restored and preserved by the John Bartram Association since the 1920s, the property offers an opportunity to see his re-created botanical gardens— the first in the New World. The gardens are open seven days a week from 10:00 A.M. to 5:00 P.M. and the house Tuesday–Sunday noon to 4:00 P.M. The site is entered from Lindbergh Boulevard above 54th Street.

### 92. Clark House

*Andrews, Jacques, and Rantouil, from Henry Hobson Richardson's office, c. 1889*

*Clark House*

The varied architectural styles, sites, and materials of the houses and churches of the West Philadelphia suburb parallel the Woodlands cemetery markers. In their variety, they tell of the American search for personal distinction as represented by possessions. Andrew Jackson Downing, writing in 1851 about *The Architecture of Country Houses* foresaw the role of style and architectural character as a means of expressing the personality of the owner; after the Centennial, architecture critic Martha Lamb used the printing metaphor of a house being like a "mold to the type" of the person who commissioned the project. Penn's neighborhood had many such individually commissioned houses on large properties. Of the few that survive such as the Clarence Clark, Jr. House at 4200 Spruce Street, most are now adapted as apartment houses. The Clark House, which stood across the street from the parental estate, was designed in the 1880s by Andrews, Jacques, and Rantouil, the young architects in Henry Hobson Richardson's office. It is a powerful example of that office's characteristic simplified Romanesque revival work.

*Ronald McDonald House*

## 93. Ronald McDonald House  *William Decker, 1893*

Another house of similar magnitude is the Ronald McDonald House at 3925 Chestnut Street, again showing the influence of Richardson. Designed by William Decker for hardware magnate William Swain in 1893, it has found a remarkable use as a short-term residence for families whose children need the care of the Children's Hospital.

## 94. 4210-20 Spruce Street  *Hewitt Brothers, c. 1885*

*4210–20 Spruce Street*

Adjacent to the Clark House at 4210–20 Spruce Street is a splendid row of urban mansions built in the mid-1880s from designs by the Hewitt Brothers, for builder William Kimball. Kimball was an in-law of the Clarks and was responsible for many of the houses in the immediate area. Despite being built as a row, the angled corner bays and the ornamented central gable indi-vidualize the houses in the manner that car manufacturers would later use to "customize" automobiles.

*Woodland Terrace*

### 95. Woodland Terrace *Samuel Sloan, 1861*

Similar individualization was achieved before the centennial in developer-built blocks of houses such as Woodland Terrace. They were constructed in 1861 between Woodland and Baltimore avenues from designs of Samuel Sloan, the author of some of the most widely circulated architectural pattern books of the pre–Civil War years. On Woodland Terrace, he designed symmetrical terraces of large Italianate semi-detached houses that give the appearance of being single houses. They alternate between brownstone and ruled and jointed stucco that is intended to imitate Ashlar masonry.

### 96. 200 Block of South 42nd Street *John Jones, 1868*

Another important Civil War–era group are the houses on the 200 block of South 42nd Street. They formed a similarly symmetrical composition with towered single houses at each end (only the northernmost of which survives) flanking mansarded twin houses of considerable size. Designed in the 1860s by John Jones, these attest to the wealth of the initial street car suburb even during the Civil War.

*St. Mark's Square*

## 97. 42nd Street Between Locust and Walnut Streets
*Hewitt Brothers, 1878*

Further north, between Locust and Walnut streets along 42nd Street is a
remarkable hierarchically organized group of houses that is attributed to the
Hewitt Brothers shortly after they split with Frank Furness. Facing 42nd
Street are pairs of brick Victorian twins with vigorously shaped chimneys
and textured gables; on Walnut Street are even larger twins faced with marble and brownstone slabs. Along St. Marks Square in the interior of the
block are two rows of neat porch-fronted brick houses accented with bands
of black bricks. They have long been the home of Penn faculty members.
This type of development became something of a commonplace in West
Philadelphia, owing to the ready availability of land and the broadly based
desire for home ownership. Willis G. Hale, Furness's chief competitor in the
1880s, designed one such group at 39th and Walnut streets. Its four-story
twins, which faced Walnut Street, have been demolished but the northern
European-influenced row of houses on the west side of 39th Street below
Sansom Street and the accompanying row of smaller houses on the south
side of Sansom Street survive.

## 98. West of 43rd Street

West of 43rd Street many of the houses are built with an elongated tan brick with dark spots—called Pompeian brick for its resemblance to Roman brick; the pressed metal ornament and cast detail on porches are indicators of the consumer culture made possible by the wealth generated by the great factories of the city. While most of the houses are not individually remarkable, the vast number of these splendidly detailed houses tells of the rising wages made possible by industrial standardization and scientific management. Powelton, north of Market Street between 32nd and 38th streets, shows houses of similar vintage and style in a neighborhood that spans from the Civil War to the end of the nineteenth century.

## 99. Garden Court

*Garden Court Plaza*

Beyond 46th Street is Garden Court, an early twentieth-century automobile suburb. By World War I, the typical Philadelphian already had a car or planned to have one shortly. Its developer, Clarence Siegel, planned the region around regional transportation systems. Apartment houses were located along Pine Street where residents could walk to the Market Street subway, while the more distant zone to the south was built for those with automobiles. Cars were incorporated into the planning by placing garages in the backs of houses. The crowning building was the Garden Court Plaza at 47th and Pine streets. It was designed in 1929 by Ralph Bencker, the successor to William Price, whose Philadelphia office pioneered the style that came to be called art deco. Four pairs of towers were planned around a central garage whose roof formed a raised landscaped plaza for residents. The Depression ended the project with only one of the pairs of towers and a portion of the garage completed.

**Tabernacle Presbyterian Church** *T. P. Chandler, 1883*
**Episcopal Church of the Saviour** *Charles Burns, 1902*
**Roman Catholic Church of Saint James and Saint Agatha**
     *Edwin Forrest Durang, 1881*
**Church of the Redeemer Presbyterian Church** *Charles Burns, c. 1880*
**St. Francis de Sales** *Henry Dagit, 1907*

*Episcopal Church of the Saviour*

Interspersed throughout Penn's neighborhood are churches whose varied denominations denote the origins of the people who settled the city. At 37th and Chestnut streets is T. P. Chandler's handsome Gothic design for the Tabernacle Presbyterian Church (see North Campus). Just north of Chestnut Street on 38th Street is Charles Burns's masterpiece, the Episcopal Church of the Saviour, which now functions as the cathedral of the local diocese. The congregation's first building was by Samuel Sloan, the architect of many of the cottages of the horsecar suburb. It was replaced in 1889 by a church by Burns, which was destroyed by fire in 1902. Burns then designed the present building, which recollects the general Italian Romanesque character of its predecessor. Added to the earlier design are a grand Lombard Romanesque tower and an extraordinary hammer-beam ceiling over the nave. The apse is decorated with a glorious cycle of murals painted by Edwin Blashfield. These were commissioned to honor the memory of Anthony J. Drexel, whose family worshiped here. The carved altar by R. Tait McKenzie is a World War I memorial, an *ara pacis* of modern soldiers. The leaded glass windows were repaired and lighted by former members of the choir, singers, and film stars Jeanette MacDonald and Nelson Eddy.

Its neighbor at the corner of 38th and Chestnut streets is the flamboyant Roman Catholic Church of Saint James and Saint Agatha. It was constructed between 1881 and 1887 from designs of Edwin Forrest Durang, the leading architect for Roman Catholic buildings after the Civil War. Here, Durang followed a more or less French Gothic design, which is most obvious in the central portal and windows of the main facade. Originally, one tower was cylindrical and the other square in plan as if built in multiple stages. That feature was undone in a later renovation. Within, the church is a riot of color that reflects the traditions of Catholic churches of the city. The massive columns of the nave colonnade are of cast iron enameled to imitate granite.

The number of Episcopal churches attests to the wealth and social status of West Philadelphia. St. Mary's Church on Locust Walk has been dealt with in Super Block (West Campus); another small gem by Charles Burns was the Church of St. Philip (c. 1882) at 42nd Street and Baltimore Avenue—now the Church of the Redeemer Presbyterian Church. Its polychromed brick and stone walls recall William Butterfield's brilliant Victorian Gothic churches of London. The parish house of 1889 with its corner tower is the work of the Hewitt Brothers. They had become the principal architects for the later developers of the neighborhood and also designed the row of 1880s twin brick Queen Anne houses that stand directly across 42nd Street.

Another landmark in the community is the glittering yellow-and-white glazed tile dome of the Byzantine-style church for the Roman Catholic congregation of St. Francis de Sales. It looms above its site at 47th and Springfield Avenue. Erected from the plans of Henry Dagit in 1907, its interior is spanned by a Gustavino tile vault that sits on four massive piers. To meet the demands of the Vatican council for closer proximity between the service and the congregation, Robert Venturi's elegant hanging neon tube excised the distant altar while preserving it for future generations.

## 101. Twentieth-Century Landmarks

### Thirtieth Street Station
*Graham, Anderson, Probst and White, 1925, restoration Dan Peter Koppel Associates with the Clio Group, Inc., 1990*
### United States Post Office *Tilden, Register, and Pepper, and Rankin and Kellogg, 1931*
### Office Blocks of the Philadelphia Evening Bulletin
*George Howe and Montgomery Brown, 1953*

In a city only rarely given to heroic gestures, three twentieth-century landmarks are clustered near the university at the gateway to West Philadelphia. On the west banks of the Schuylkill River, three eighteenth-century great roads, Woodland Avenue from the southwest and Market Street and Lancaster Avenue from the west, converged at the Market Street ferry. The ferry was later replaced by the first permanent bridge across the river in 1800, further cementing its importance as a center for transportation. Over the next century, railroads followed the east and west banks of the river, in turn attracting the abattoirs, warehouses, and factories that made the region an industrial zone. In the twentieth century, these utilitarian buildings gave way to the Pennsylvania Railroad's plan for a grand entrance into the city over the intercity lines that ran along the Schuylkill River.

*Thirtieth Street Station*

The first building of the group to be constructed was Thirtieth Street Station—now the principal intercity terminal of AMTRAK and the hub of the region's commuter railroads. It was designed for the Pennsylvania Railroad in 1925 by Graham, Anderson, Probst and White, successors to Daniel Burnham's Chicago office. Its five-story hall is classical in detail, but the hot orange and gold highlights are Roaring Twenties. The station was restored and a food court was added to the side wings in 1991 by Dan Peter Koppel Associates with the Clio Group, Inc.

Across Market Street is the massive bulk of the city's principal United States Post Office, which was sited above the principal intercity rail lines. Its architects, Tilden, Register, and Pepper designed the Mahoney wing of the University Hospital in Penn's palette of materials. Here the limestone cladding parallels the railroad station. The Mayan art deco styling of the exterior and the brilliant marble revetments of the postal gallery at the east end are hallmarks of its early 1930s date. The third building of the group is the moderne office block of the *Philadelphia Evening Bulletin* at 31st Street, which was designed by Montgomery Brown and George Howe, the famed modern architect of the PSFS skyscraper. Here Brown and Howe used a neutral gray brick and rounded corners carried on stainless steel-clad pilotis to grapple with the conventions of Euro-modernism, while attaining the monumentality of its neighbors. The building now houses divisions of the city archives, as well as remote storage for Penn's library.

## 102. Drexel University

**Main Building** *Wilson Brothers, 1889*
**Paul Peck Center** *Frank Furness, 1876, addition Voith and McTavish, 1999*

*Drexel University Main Building*

Between the landmarks of 30th Street and the university is the campus of Drexel University. Drexel's Main Building at 32nd and Chestnut streets is a tour de force of turn-of-the-century design by the Wilson Brothers—the region's and the nation's principal architecture and engineering firm after the centennial. Joseph Wilson had trained at Rensselaer Polytechnic Institute, studied metallurgy at the University of Pennsylvania, and then directed the bridge design group for the Pennsylvania Railroad. When he formed his own office in 1876, there were few who could match his technical brilliance or experience. Wilson had the trust of Anthony Drexel, designing his downtown bank as well as the house of one of his children. In 1889 when Drexel conceived of establishing a technical institute, he commissioned Joseph Wilson to visit similar European schools, devise the curriculum, and then design the building that would house the new school.

Wilson designed a splendid skylight-covered interior court like an Italian palazzo that is flanked on the main level by the library and administrative offices; a large auditorium spans the rear of the building. Classrooms on the upper levels opened onto single loaded corridors that surround the great interior atrium. The exterior is clad in yellow brick ornamented with cast terra-cotta and organized by regularly spaced piers that represent the underlying structure of iron columns. The main entrance off Chestnut Street is framed by terra-cotta busts of geniuses in the arts and sciences, including Michelangelo for sculpture, Bach for music, William of Sens (the French architect of Canterbury Cathedral) for architecture, and Faraday for science. The eastern wing continues the palette of materials but reflects the baroque scale of the Chicago Fair; it is also by the Wilson Brothers in 1901.

Drexel's other landmark is Frank Furness's mini-masterpiece for centennial-era visitors, the Centennial Bank. Its beveled main facade manages simultaneously to confront 32nd Street, Lancaster Avenue, Market Street, and Woodland Avenue. Cleaned of a century of accumulated dirt,

*Paul Peck Center*

and with its interior returned to its original brilliant pattern of polychromed brick, it is now one of the most complete of Furness's early masterpieces. Renamed the Paul Peck Center after its 1999 restoration, it now houses Drexel's art gallery. An awkwardly detailed addition by Voith and McTavish attempts to compete with Furness's vigorous manner while ignoring the obvious Furness hierarchy. Nearby buildings on Drexel's campus look as if they took their cues from Penn's orange brick Rittenhouse Laboratory. A new dormitory by Michael Graves at 33rd above Arch Street brings strong color and clear shapes and patterns to bear and suggests that Drexel's future designs may be better than those of its recent past.

# *Bibliography*

*General Histories*

Boorstin, Daniel J. *The Americans: The Colonial Experience*. New York: Vintage Books, 1958.

Canby, Henry Seidel. *American Memoir*. Boston: Houghton Mifflin Company, 1947.

Fischer, David Hackett. *Albion's Seed: Four British Folkways in America*. New York: Oxford University Press, 1989.

Rudolf, Frederick. *The American College and University: A History*. New York: A. Knopf, 1961.


*Philadelphia: Social and Cultural History*

Baltzell, E. Digby. *Philadelphia Gentlemen: The Making of a National Upper Class*. New York: Free Press, 1958.

———*Puritan Boston and Quaker Philadelphia: Two Protestant Ethics and the Spirit of Class Authority and Leadership*. New York: Free Press, 1979.

Burt, Nathaniel. *The Perennial Philadelphians*. Boston: Little, Brown and Co. 1963.

Franklin, Benjamin. *Autobiography*. Ed. Larzer Ziff. New York: Holt, Rinehart, and Winston, 1959.

Kalm, Peter. *Travels in North America*, John R. Forster, trans. London, 1770; reprint, New York: Dover, 1987.

Larabee, Leonard. *The Papers of Benjamin Franklin*. New Haven: Yale University Press, 1965.

Mease, James M.D. *The Picture of Philadelphia as it is in 1811*. Philadelphia: B & T. Kite, 1811.

Scharf, J. Thomas and Thomas Westcott. *History of Philadelphia 1609–1884*. 3 vols. Philadelphia: L. H. Everts & Co. 1884.

Warner, Sam Bass. *Philadelphia: The Private City*. Philadelphia: University of Pennsylvania Press, 1966.

Weigley, Russell, ed. *Philadelphia: A 300-Year History*. New York: W.W. Norton and Co., 1982.


*Architectural and Design History*

Bendiner, Albert. *Bendiner's Philadelphia*. New York: A.S. Barnes and Co. 1964.

Cram, Ralph Adams. "The Work of Messrs. Frank Miles Day and Brother." *Architectural Record* 15, no. 3 (May 1904): 397.

———"The Work of Cope and Stewardson." *Architectural Record* 15, no. 5 (November 1904): 407–438.

Edgell, George. *The American Architecture of Today.* New York: Charles Scribner's Sons, 1928.

Elliot, Huger. "Architecture in Philadelphia." *Architectural Record* 23 (April 1908): 294 ff.

Gilchrist, Agnes Addison. *William Strickland: Architect and Engineer, 1788–1855.* Philadelphia: University of Pennsylvania Press, 1950.

Green, Wilder. "Louis I. Kahn: Richards Medical Research Building." *Museum of Modern Art Bulletin* 28 (1961).

Kelsey, Albert. *The Architectural Annual* 1 Philadelphia: The Architectural Annual, 1901.

Klauder, Charles Z. and Herbert C. Wise. *College Architecture in America.* New York: Charles Scribner's Sons, 1929.

Kurjack, Dennis C. "Who Designed the President's House." *Journal of the Society of Architectural Historians* 12 (May 1953): 27–28.

Laird, Warren Powers. "Records of a Consulting Practice" 62 (unpublished typescript, Rare Book Room, Fisher Fine Arts Library, University of Pennsylvania): 1–4.

Martin, Sidney. "Architectural Elements of the New Campus." *General Magazine and Historical Chronicle.* (Winter 1952): 65.

Millard, Julian. "The Work of Wilson Eyre." *Architectural Record.* 14, no. 4 (October 1903): 280–325.

Schuyler, Montgomery. "The Architecture of American Colleges, V. University of Pennsylvania, Girard, Haverford, Lehigh and Bryn Mawr Colleges." *Architectural Record* 28 (July–December 1910): 183 ff.

Sewell, Darrell, ed. *Philadelphia: Three Centuries of American Art.* Philadelphia: Philadelphia Museum of Art, 1976.

Snyder, Martin. *City of Independence: Maps and Views of Philadelphia before 1800.* New York: Praeger Publishers, 1975.

Strong, Ann and George E. Thomas. *The Book of the School: 100 Years of the Graduate School of Fine Arts.* Philadelphia: Graduate School of Fine Arts, 1991.

Tatman, Sandra and Roger Moss. *Biographical Dictionary of Philadelphia Architecture, 1700–1930.* Boston: G. K. Hall, 1985.

Taylor, Frederick Winslow. "Address." *Publication of the University of Pennsylvania, Proceedings of the Dedication of the New Building for the Engineering Department, October 19, 1906.* Philadelphia: University of Pennsylvania, 1906.

Thomas, George, et. al. *Frank Furness: The Complete Works.* New York: Princeton Architectural Press, 1991.

Turner, Paul V. *Campus: An American Planning Tradition.* Cambridge, MA: MIT Press, 1984.

Van Horne, John. *The Papers of Benjamin Henry Latrobe, Correspondence and Miscellaneous Papers, 1805–10.* New Haven: Yale University Press, 1986.

Westcott, Thompson. *Historical Mansions of Philadelphia.* Philadelphia: Porter and Coates, 1877.

Williams, Talcott. "Plans for the Library of the University of Pennsylvania." *Library Journal* (August 13, 1888): 237–43.


*University of Pennsylvania Master Plans*

Adelman, Collins, and Dutot. "Open Space and Beautification Program, University City," Philadelphia, 1966.

Center for Environmental Design and Planning. "A Master Plan for the Campus." *Almanac* supplement May 17, 1988.

Cret, Paul, P. et al. "Report to the Board of Trustees of the University of Pennsylvania Upon the Future Development of Buildings and Grounds and the Conservation of Surrounding Territory." Philadelphia: Privately Published, 1913.

Davis and Brody, "University of Pennsylvania Master Plan," 1979.

Olin Partnership, "Campus Development Plan," 1999.

Philadelphia City Planning, "University City Core Plan," 1966.

Shepheard, Peter, et al. *Landscape Development Plan.* Philadelphia: University of Pennsylvania, 1977.

University of Pennsylvania Planning Office, "University of Pennsylvania Development Plan," 1961, 1963. 1966.


*University of Pennsylvania–related Histories*

Cheyney, Edward Potts. *History of the University of Pennsylvania, 1740–1940.* Philadelphia, 1940.

Cooper, David, III and Marshall Ledger. *Innovation and Tradition at the University of Pennsylvania Medical School.* Philadelphia: University of Pennsylvania Press, 1990.

Corner, George W. *Two Centuries of Medicine: A History of the School of Medicine of the University of Pennsylvania.* Philadelphia: J.B. Lippincott Co. 1965.

Dunn, Richard and Mark F. Lloyd, eds. *A Pennsylvania Album; Undergraduate Essays on the 250th Anniversary of the University of Pennsylvania.* Philadelphia: University of Pennsylvania, 1990: 31–37.

Geggenheimer, Albert. *William Smith: Educator and Churchman.*
Philadelphia: University of Pennsylvania Press, 1943.

General Alumni Society. *The University of Pennsylvania: A Glimpse of the
Campus.* Philadelphia, 1914.

Goshorn, Robert. "The Valley Forge Project of the University of
Pennsylvania," *Tredyffrin Easttown History Club Quarterly* 24, no.1
(January 1986): 17–34.

Harrison, Charles Custis "Autobiography" ms. University of Pennsylvania
Archives.

——"Memoirs," University of Pennsylvania Archives.

——et al, *University of Pennsylvania: The Dormitory System*, Philadelphia:
Edward Stern & Co., 1895

——"The Class of '62." *General Magazine and Historical Chronicle* 1927–8:
341.

Hottel, Althea. "The Women of Pennsylvania," *Gazette* 55, no. 6 (February
1957): 8 ff.

Lippincott, H. Mather. "The Problem of a College in a City." *General
Magazine and Historical Chronicle*, XXVIII: 4 (July 1926): 437 ff.

McMaster, John B. *The University of Pennsylvania Illustrated.* Philadelphia:
J.B. Lippincott, 1897.

Maxwell, W. J. *General Alumni Catalogue of the University of Pennsylvania.*
1917 Philadelphia: University of Pennsylvania Alumni Association,
1917.

Meyerson, Martin and Dilys Pegler Winegrad, *Gladly Learn and Gladly
Teach, Franklin and his heirs at the University of Pennsylvania.*
Philadelphia: University of Pennsylvania Press, 1978.

Montgomery, Thomas Harrison. *A History of the University of Pennsylvania.*
Philadelphia: George W. Jacobs & Co., 1900.

Nitzsche, George. *The University of Pennsylvania Illustrated.* Philadelphia:
1906.

Oberholtzer, Ellis Paxon, "Charles C. Harrison," steel plate supplement,
*Philadelphia, Pictorial and Biographical.* Philadelphia: S. J. Clarke
Publishing Co., 1911.

Smith, Edgar Fahs. *The Life of Robert Hare.* Philadelphia: J. B. Lippincott
Co., 1917.

Spiller, Robert E. "The Valley Forge Project." *General Magazine and
Historical Chronicle*, XXIX (4 July 1927): 457 ff.

Stillé, Charles. *Reminiscences of a Provost.* Philadelphia: 1880.

Thomas, George E. and David B. Brownlee. *Building America's First
University: An Historical and Architectural Guide to the University of
Pennsylvania.* Philadelphia: University of Pennsylvania Press, 2000.

Thorpe, Francis N. *Benjamin Franklin and His University.* Washington D.C.,
1893.

Turner, William C. "The College, Academy, and Charitable School of
    Philadelphia: the Development of a Colonial Institution of
    Learning." Ph.D. diss. University of Pennsylvania, 1952.
——"The Charity School, the Academy, and the College," *Historic
    Philadelphia from the Founding until the Nearly Nineteenth Century*,
    Luther Eisenhart, ed., *Transactions of the American Philosophical
    Society* vol. 43, part 1 (Philadelphia, 1953): 179–186.
Wood, George. *Early History of the University of Pennsylvania*. Philadelphia:
    J. B. Lippincott, 1896.

# *Illustration Credits*

Unless noted below, all photographs are copyright 2002 © Lewis Tanner.

pp. v bottom left and right, viii, ix, x, 28, 31, 37, 42, 58, 59 top, 60, 62 bottom,
    63 right, 66, 67, 69, 72 top and bottom, 84 top, 86 top and bottom,
    89, 90, 91, 92, 93, 96, 98 left, 106 bottom, 109, 116, 120, 121, 122, 123,
    124, 130, 131, 132 top and bottom, 137, 142 bottom, 144, 148, 149 bot-
    tom, 152, 153, 155, 156, 158, 159 bottom, 160, 174, 175 bottom, 176, 177,
    178, 179, 183, 184: George E. Thomas, photographer
pp. xv, 65 bottom: Courtesy MGA Partners, Barry Halkin photographer
pp. xvi, 1, 5, 6, 7, 10, 12 left and right, 16, 19, 20, 21: University Archives
pp. 3, 9, 18: George E. Thomas Collection
p. 23: University of Pennsylvania Facilities Office
pp. 41, 47: Venturi, Scott Brown, and Associates, Matt Wargo, photographer
    (41); Julie Marquart, photographer (47)
p. 71: Thomas W. Shaller, del. for Kohn, Pedersen Fox Associates
p. 84 bottom: Courtesy Kieran Timberlake Associates
pp. 97, 164 bottom: Courtesy Atkin, Ohshin, Lawson-Bell Associates,
    Catharine Tighe photographer (97)
p. 104: Courtesy John Milner Architects
p. 111: Courtesy Leers Weinzapfel Associates
p. 162: Courtesy Bohlin, Cywinski, Jackson Architects
p. 164 top: Courtesy Wood and Zapata Associates

# *Index*